THE SMART GIRLS HANDBOOK

THE SMART GIRLS HANDBOOK

HOW TO SILENCE SELF-DOUBT, FIND YOUR PURPOSE AND REDEFINE THE IMPOSSIBLE

SCARLETT V CLARK

The mental health & wellbeing publisher

First published in 2021
This edition published in 2023 by Trigger Publishing
An imprint of Shaw Callaghan Ltd

UK Office
The Stanley Building
7 Pancras Square
Kings Cross
London N1C 4AG

US Office
On Point Executive Center, Inc
3030 N Rocky Point Drive W
Suite 150
Tampa, FL 33607
www.triggerhub.org

A CIP catalogue record for this book is available upon request from the British Library
ISBN: 9781837963676
Ebook ISBN: 9781837963683

Cover design by Emily Courdelle
Typeset by Lapiz Digital Services

You are enough,
You are beautiful,
You are unique,
You are worthy.

Scarlett V Clark is a speaker and the award-winning founder and CEO of Smart Girl Tribe, the UK's number one female empowerment community. Scarlett uses her magnetic energy to empower women to design a life they love as their most authentic selves through her top-rated podcast, wildly successful event series, blossoming YouTube channel and activism. Scarlett regularly speaks at Harvard University as a female empowerment expert and works with UN Women, Women for Women International and HeforShe advocating for women everywhere.

CONTENTS

INTRODUCTION

Comparisons, self-doubt, expectations and pressure. I'm calling it.

Who prepares you? Who is there to support and guide you on your journey to becoming a woman? It would be so much easier if there was a number we could call for the answers, someone we could talk to who is in charge. Just to make the simple request: that it not be *so* hard.

I could easily lay out all of the issues and problems we naturally have to face growing up as a woman, and there are thousands of books out there that do. However, I want to discuss how to prevent and overcome these challenges: how to deal with panic attacks and mental health issues, what to do if you fail an exam, and the mental strength it takes to see all those perfect models on social media. These are all tragedies (for lack of a better word) that I grew up with and know you may be experiencing too.

When I started Smart Girl Tribe, #MeToo and Time's Up didn't exist. There was a need for a network that was having these important conversations, when "How To Lose 7 Pounds in 7 Days" or "How to Make Him Want You" were the headlines splashed across the magazines we were surrounded by in shops and online. The platform that was needed didn't exist. There was no outlet telling us to stop listening to the negativity around us and letting other people's opinions or our dress size define our worth. Women needed a hub that would question society and the standards we set ourselves *every single day*. Everywhere, though, I was told that: "this is just the way it is". Apparently, generations before me had faced similar pressures and the generation after me was going to as well. *Someone* had to change the system. *Someone* had to write a new narrative. *Someone* had to redefine womanhood. Then I realized, I am someone.

... Cue Smart Girl Tribe.

I am not a guidance counsellor, mentor, guru, philosopher, mother divine or a genius.

I AM JUST A GIRL WHO DECIDED TO GO FOR IT.

I began Smart Girl Tribe in my first year of university to reflect the conversations that my friends and I were hearing and having. Fundamentally believing women deserved more from the media, this is how it all began, first as a digital magazine and a community of perfectly imperfect girls learning to love themselves; by setting out to be the girl I needed growing up, the woman *you* need growing up.

At 19 years old I started my passion project, and now it is the UK's number one female empowerment organization.

I have travelled the world, written for major publications, created a top-rated podcast and a wildly successful event series, launched a membership platform, been invited to speak at Harvard University as a female empowerment expert, and visited schools and universities inspiring hundreds of thousands of young women. I have worked with UN Women, the British Council, HeforShe and been an ambassador for the NSPCC. Smart Girl Tribe has evolved into a transformative media empire which offers women an autonomous way of living, full of freedom and bursting with love.

It was during my first UK tour as a female empowerment speaker that I realized the extent of what wasn't being shared and talked about. After my speeches, women from all walks of life would queue up, waiting to talk to me. Yet, meeting young women desperate to speak with me, just for one question, made me realize how much *still* wasn't being done. I didn't want to just answer that one question and then leave you. To give you something tangible to pick up every day, I wrote this book.

We are made to thrive, not just survive, and *The Smart Girls Handbook* is full of the most vital lessons I have learned on my journey. It is divided into eight promises – promises that over the years I have made to myself, promises the Smart Girl Tribe team has made, and promises that *you* will be making after this book. In each chapter you will find a personal story of mine, an account of how I made my dreams come true and everything that went wrong in between, not forgetting my biggest and boldest mistakes. I also share the tangible actions that have helped me change my life, and exercises to support you to step forward.

This is for *you* – the messy, complicated, kind-hearted, multi-faceted, broken and adventurous you – whether you're at university, building your first business or have recently taken on a new job; if you're changing careers or are a stay-at-home mum; if you're single or in a relationship. Whether you're reading this for yourself or for your daughter, write notes in the margins, scribble in the back or, even better, pass this on to a fellow smart girl once you have finished with it.

Women are our world's untapped resource and secret weapon. I am writing for the women who send me messages and ask questions at the Smart Girl Tribe Summits, *and* for all of you who have never even heard of me until now. Disclaimer: listen to me for too long and you'll actually start believing you can achieve anything you set your mind to.

No matter where you live in the world or what you are going through, I understand the impact that mean girls can have, how loud our inner critic is, and how tough it can be to figure out what we really want from our lives. Some days you want the world to swallow you up and other days you want to take it over. Just like you, I have worried about not being funny, smart or pretty enough, and we all feel like that sometimes.

The smart girl, the one who seems to have her life together, she is already in you.

I also know what it feels like to go after your dream and not have any support, how hard it can be to change your life, and the effort of living with anxiety. How many years will have to go by until we see change? Real change. That's a conversation we are going to start having right now.

The Smart Girls Handbook is a celebration of being and becoming a woman. Bringing together inspiration, ideas, game-changing practical suggestions and words from women who have been through it all, this book is so powerful you will read it again and again.

She exists and is desperate to conquer the world. I am going to light your soul on fire and remind you how amazing you are, inspire you to not just dream big, but *do* big. Women have always been a force to be reckoned with, but how often do you *not* feel like that? Smart Girl Tribe was created to give everyone the tools they needed to excel and prosper in the modern world – imagine if this tribe really became the army the world needs.

How extraordinary would that be?

WHAT TO DO RIGHT NOW

It comes as no surprise to me that you're busy and juggling a lot, I anticipate that here lies a risk that your interest in these words won't translate to immediate action. I have two suggestions for you to enable that breakthrough right now:

SMART GIRL ACTIONS

1. Take the assessment/checklist at smartgirltribe.com to discover the areas which you need to work on to change your life today.

2. Read the first two chapters straight away. I want to ignite that dream in your heart or fire in your belly. It won't take long. Diving in and committing to reading will make that exponential difference between staying where you are right now and where you could be, being the woman you are destined to become.

THE SMART GIRL TRIBE PROMISES

Here are the promises you need to make to yourself every day in order to be your fearless and authentic self, and design the life and business or career that fills you with joy.

1. I promise to discover my talent and find my passion
2. I promise to learn how to deal with the fear of failure
3. I promise to cope with anxiety and start speaking my truth
4. I promise to slay the mean girls and build a strong tribe of true friends
5. I promise to be confident and love myself
6. I promise to be a total #Boss
7. I promise to embrace self-care and take a well-needed pause
8. I promise to stand up and help change the world

CHAPTER 1

I PROMISE TO DISCOVER MY TALENT AND FIND MY PASSION

My palms were clammy, and the fear persistent. Notes filled my hand and I was mentally preparing for last-minute changes. The spot at the front of the room had been cleared from the previous act and it was my turn in a few moments. Of course I had stayed up late the night before to prepare for this moment. The formidable pillars in the corner of the room towered over my tiny frame. The crowd was staring back at me, no doubt anticipating my first word.

I was seven years old.

This was my first public speaking gig.

It was Miss Coleman's Year 3 English lesson. We had to present our life ambitions to the class. Well, as much as you can at seven. As I enjoyed writing, I already knew that was where my life would lead me. Halfway through my presentation, the teacher peered up from her notebook and sternly insisted: "You have to say what you would *like* to be, not what you *will* be."

Under the assumption the crowd would be wildly impressed by my audacious dreams and would soon break into huge applause, I couldn't believe it. My parents had raised me on the idea that with enough willpower, anything was possible. Was someone really going to silence my aspiring words? Absolutely not. I carried on with my speech including the word "will" at every opportunity. Through sheer determination and undervalued stubbornness to prove a point, I refused to change that four-letter word.

Since then, having travelled the world as a writer, I am pretty sure that somewhere Miss Coleman knows this. At least, the seven-year-old in me hopes so. Was it easy? Heck, no.

Years later at university, students distributed the student newspaper out all over campus. I yearned to write for it but considered myself too shy and introverted to take that first step to get involved. One morning I finally plucked up the courage to head to the university's newspaper office. I didn't know how many blessings would come from it or how major a part of my life it would become, but I went for it.

Knocking on the *BathImpact* door was similar to bracing myself for take-off. A scruffy student greeted me, his sleeves were rolled up to his elbows, his dark-rimmed glasses were

Finding a passion, that is where the magic happens.

smeared and his jeans were covered in marker pen to match the stains on his hands. He ushered me in, not even asking my name, and pointed me in the direction of the editor. Kylie, the editor, had flaming red hair and an obvious sense of self which I admired. She was warm but direct. After a quick chat she assigned me my first article.

Despite the initial worry, writing for *BathImpact* throughout my university years was one of the best experiences of my life, and it is probably thanks to that time that I am now writing this book. See – you never know when and how your passion is going to find you.

Your passion is something you love to do, something you would do happily for free and forever.

In life, some things are inevitable – such as taxes, ageing and earning a living. Without a passion in your life, those obligations can cage you and hold you down. Passion is where you will find community, connection, fulfilment and joy.

In this chapter, I'm going to show you how to embark on the rollercoaster ride to identify your passion, and what to do once you've found it. I'm not just going to unleash you into a world of random hobbies and pursuits here though. There are three steps you need to take to find your passion and live it out. I want you to look out for it, show up for it and ignore everything else.

"Passion is energy. Feel the power that comes from focusing on what excites you."

— Oprah Winfrey

FIND YOUR PASSION

One of the most popular questions I get messaged or emailed is: "How do I find it, though – that passion or purpose?"

Realizing what your passion is can be a huge undertaking. I hear you. You're probably thinking, *good for you*. You knew what you wanted even before it became necessary to know, or even expected of you. What about me? In reality it took years of stumbling around to fully recognize what I enjoy naturally. Just because you haven't found it yet doesn't mean that it doesn't exist.

One thing is certain – before you embark on this journey towards finding your passion, you need to begin with the right perspective. If you believe that you don't have a passion, or doubt you will find it, then you won't. It's similar to when you go shopping needing to find a particular outfit but convinced you won't, and unsurprisingly, it doesn't appear.

Be positive and look for the clues to your passion around you. For most of us, our passion is a joy. We radiate positive energy when we're busy with our passion, we feel closer to our authentic self and more in balance in life. Our passion might be something worth fighting for – connected to our intrinsic values. Perhaps a belief or political party that riles us so badly we can't help but share our views, an injustice we want to draw attention to, a cause we need to fight for.

Think about what you already love to do. Are you a creative type? Is your dream to dance? Or to sky-dive? Know that your passion will make your heart sing; it will all-consume you and you won't be able to switch off from it, because you won't want to. It might be blogging or becoming a make-up artist, surfing or teaching someone how to draw – you are going to love your passion so much you won't ever want to stop.

Marie Forleo is an American entrepreneur and bestselling author. She had a passion for business and for dance, so guess what? She not only became a Nike Elite Dance Athlete but a top selling fitness DVD creator. Mixing her passions for dance and business. Or take *me*, I have a passion for business and writing so I created a digital magazine, meshing together my two loves. Your passion might bring together different interests or elements, and this could take time to fully understand.

Sometimes we can get so caught up in everything we are already doing that we forget to ask ourselves if what we're pursuing is actually making us happy. Trying new pastimes refreshes our thinking and fosters our sense of what is important to us and what we connect with. Keep looking and trying to identify ideas and themes that resonate with you.

Or until they find you. For now, not knowing what you want to do is okay, more than okay. For 18 years you are told what to do. Your school timetable is decided for you, your subjects are given to you and someone else even gets to choose who sits next to you. Then, suddenly, you have to start making those big decisions, those huge choices that are going to shape the rest of your life. We are set up to go along with what we are told to do – it's good to challenge the life you're living, to question if it is what you really want.

...Insert the beep here.

EXERCISE: RATE YOUR PASSIONS

Rating your interests and hobbies is a great way to dig into what truly energizes you. Start by listing your current passions and pastimes, and take time over the list. Ensure that you include new interests and talents as well as those activities you enjoyed in childhood, or that thing you keep meaning to try. Then, next to each one, score how meaningful each item is to you. Maybe your tennis lessons on a Saturday aren't so enjoyable and score as low as

2 or 3, whereas your interest in wildlife conservation is important to you and scores a 7 or 8. The activities that score low you should consider clearing out of your diary; if it's not sparking joy then leave it to someone else to take up.

This exercise won't only help you realize what activities are the most or least valued by you, it is also a tool to help you identify and understand the skills, talents and gifts you have – look for similarities and themes across the high-scoring items on your list. Use this exercise to find the space in your calendar to add in new activities and bring more meaning to your life.

Maybe your friend has the same hobby as you – after all, that's how you meet or bond with people you like. There are millions of women and a ton of them are going to be taking on something similar to you, but nobody can do exactly what you can. Your passion is unique to you because nobody will have the same experience or set of skills and talents as you.

Ask your friends and family what they think you enjoy or are competent at. They might have some great evidence and ideas that haven't even occurred to you. Why not ask to tag along to some of the activities that interest them? Even if you hate your aunt's Spanish classes or cheering on your cousin at her rugby game, at least you'll realize what your passion definitely isn't – and seeing others immersed in their own pursuits could remind you of times when you have felt similarly inspired. Your current or former boss or lecturers might also have some great advice and tips, or even clubs they think would be useful for you to attend.

Look out for your passion by exploring local offerings and compiling research. Investigate events or festivals happening near you, and see what appeals. If you're apprehensive about going alone, then call a friend and invite them to join you.

If you are at university there will be a huge range of societies to try. Find out what clubs are accepting new members – in my experience, university clubs are always looking for new students to join. Or find out what is going on in the city centre, away from your campus. During my higher education, my friend Kate was part of a ballet class happening in the city centre. Even though our university offered a range of ballet classes and for all different levels, she was eager to meet new people, and ultimately she loved every minute.

When you're working, it can be harder. Use Google to find out what is happening in your local area or if there are any clubs publicized in the building where you work. Remember that there are also lots of free groups to join online to connect with like-minded individuals. I'm an active member of a "coffee and chat" group that comes together over Zoom every Monday morning for a couple of hours. It is a group video call my friend hosts, so head on over to Eventbrite and check out anything similar happening. I have also joined various book clubs over the years, depending on where I am living. There is also the Smart Girl Tribe society which is a membership platform and free Facebook group; it is a collective for millennials and female entrepreneurs to connect, grow and build a business.

At this point, it's important not to worry about your passion being financially viable. You don't need to make money from your passion at this stage, you just need to find the thing that flicks your switch and makes you happy.

As simple as it would be to have someone knock on your door to let you know what your passion is, that's just not going to happen. *You* have to be the one on the look-out for it. You have no other choice. If you want to grasp your best life, you are going to need to go after it.

SHOW UP FOR IT

Next, you need to start showing up for your passion, or for the chance to uncover your dreams. You are surrounded by opportunities every day but I bet you turn down more than you participate in. Imagine you decline a party invitation because you don't know anyone, yet at that party you could meet a future client or new friend, a fellow businesswoman or even an investor, but you'll never know because you didn't go. It will always be easier to turn something down. It's never too late, though, to start making purposeful choices. Just take the first step and say "yes".

Connections and meetings are great ways to extend your circle and expose yourself to new ideas. Networking can help you reach even more people and get better informed, which can lead to new prospects and greater chances. It's no wonder that 85% of positions are filled through networking. You might have noticed that I have interviewed a range of talented women on our podcast, from bestselling author Jennifer Nadel and conflict photographer Alison Baskerville to renowned viral poet Aija Mayrock and activist Rahila Gupta. Guess where I met all of these women? Yes – at events, which have in turn led to other opportunities, for them and for me.

You also show up for your dream by making sacrifices. To indulge in your passion you might need to let go of other activities, such as spending a Saturday morning in bed or using social media as a distraction for hours each day. Family connections haven't been the secret to my success, nor has celebrity status or lots of money. I am the hardest working person at my passion. I'm a hustler – I look for connections, make opportunities, and I constantly work at it. When I started

Smart Girl Tribe, hustling meant rising before the sun and accepting that my bedroom was an office with a bed in it. It was calling hundreds of organizations to discuss partnering with them to hear one yes. I wrote content at 5am and stayed up late shooting photos. Hustling was hiring a van to transport the SGT merchandise for my talks, and saying yes to networking events even though the introvert in me wanted to hide. Hustling meant working on the ground every day, taking baby steps which together moved me towards my dream. I've missed a lot of parties and gigs, cosy nights in and lazy weekends away because I wanted to make my time work for me.

Look through your calendar and circle any unnecessary activities you are wasting time on. Turn on the screen time evaluator if you have a smartphone so you can actually see how many hours you are wasting on social media. Now dedicate those extra hours to your passion or finding out what it is. Remember, you aren't losing anything important, you are gaining your best self and investing in your future.

Showing up for it also means not living out someone else's dream or ambition chosen for you, not by you. You are the only one who can write your life story, so make it an epic one, full of your own choices, mistakes and adventures. Don't settle for mediocre passions or the dreams that make your friends, or even your parents, feel alive.

Value your time, invest in yourself and think about where your energy is being spent.

Making your family proud or doing what is expected of you means that you might not be fully onboard with exploring your passion. Family dynamics can be complicated, and as much as we love our family, they can also drive us up the wall. Don't stop following your dream for someone else. Ask yourself what you need to do in order to live your best life.

Inspired by Nicholas Murray Butler, I like to say: "There are three types of people in the world; those who make things happen; those who don't; and, lastly, those who wondered what the heck happened?" Who are you going to be? You're not going to find your passion without getting out, I can assure you.

KEEP ON MOVING FORWARD

There are thousands of women who could be in my position. The difference between me and them is that every time I have come up against a roadblock when chasing my passion, I haven't listened. Nothing has come easy to me, and because of that I have never hesitated when someone has said "no", and never given up on the countless times I have been rejected. I've heard the word "no" so many times it's almost sounded like a "yes". If you can't get through the front door then try the side window, and if the window is locked then shimmy down the chimney. Where there is a will, there is a way.

It is hard to dream big. When building Smart Girl Tribe, friends of mine were securing promotions at work, getting married, having babies and buying houses. Those are the days when you have to remember why you started.

Nothing that is worth having happens quickly, and nothing that happens quickly is worth having. Dreams do not have expiration dates. Julia Child was 49 years old when she changed cooking in America, Susan Boyle was 48 when she appeared on *Britain's Got Talent* and found fame. Comedian Kristen Wiig didn't start delivering all those SNL zingers until she was in her mid-thirties and Reese Witherspoon launched her media company Hello Sunshine at 40. If you don't keep going, someone will keep going instead of you.

There is no escalator to success, it is a stairway. You will have to climb up step after step after step. You'll get tired, trip and fall down. People will push you off, or help you up and then push you off again. If you keep moving upwards and moving around the obstacles and avoid looking backwards/downwards, you *will* reach the top.

LIFE PURPOSE

I think it's important to note that your passion might be your purpose in life, and it also might not. Smart Girl Tribe started as my passion project. I had a dream to support young women and offering them an alternative life; over time lifting women up and empowering them has become my purpose.

Your passion might be a side hustle that you have no desire to make your purpose. Your passion is about you – what you enjoy, what you love. Your purpose is the reason you believe you are here on the planet, what you can give to others. Don't worry if you don't feel you have found your purpose yet; sometimes it won't come to you until later in life and that's okay. Gwyneth Paltrow was a hugely successful actress but felt she had a higher calling; it was at 35 that she launched Goop. Acting is her passion but Goop is her calling.

Don't tear yourself up about your purpose – start with your passion, the dream in your heart, and keep assessing how you are best qualified to show up for others. When your passion and purpose are aligned, that is when you will truly perform as your best self.

STAY STRONG

Your passion isn't going to arrive wrapped up in a pretty package either. You have to unapologetically grab it, hold on to it, and be prepared to ignore any negativity coming your way. This is probably the raddest piece of advice I can give you . . . ready? Nobody will fight for your dream as much as you can. Your friends won't; not your parents, your partner or even your great-grandmother, because no one will ever care about it as much as you do.

Perhaps a friend or a partner is trying to keep you tethered to the ground, or maybe someone in an authoritative position is saying "no", telling you you're not right for it. If someone says you are too young or suggests that you're too female or not the "right" person, don't give up. Don't let other people's opinions be another reason to quit on yourself, or your dreams. No arguments.

When it comes to negative people, you need to mentally expel them from your thoughts. If they try to suck the positive energy from you, work to compartmentalize them and just nod at what they say. Don't give them airtime. Remember that your passion and/or purpose doesn't need to make sense to anyone else but *you*.

Discovering your purpose and how you can contribute to the world in a unique way is going to make you feel alive. Would you rather live a life you choose or a life someone else has chosen for you? You'll never be happy if you just listen to what everyone else wants you to do. You have to know in your heart not to give up on yourself or your dream. No passion is worth sacrificing for someone else's opinion.

EXERCISE: THE 5-5-5 RULE

If you have been following me for a while, you will know about my 5-5-5 activity. Each day I carve out some time to write in my Smart Girl Tribe journal.

I list five goals I have in my life. Knowing nobody else will see my list, I let myself dream big. My goals have previously included speaking at Harvard, having a published book and completing a master's in journalism, all of which have come true.

After writing my five dreams, I choose the one I am currently focusing on and next to it write the five steps required to get closer to where I want to be. This is a fantastic method to track progress. So if you want to write and have a book published too, then one step for the day might be to write 1,000 words towards that target, or to call a friend who has connections with a literary agent to ask their advice. Perhaps it's as simple as to set up a daily writing hour in your schedule for the next month.

Maybe your dream is to become a personal trainer, in which case your daily tasks might include research into niche areas of fitness/health that appeal to you, working on a personal skill that will help you to become a highly motivational and effective trainer or developing a social media plan for yourself.

These five steps aren't just to stare at. Use them as a map – because, triber, a goal without a plan will only ever stay a dream. Writing down your five goals doesn't mean that you need to go after them all at once, but seeing them on paper will at least give you clarity. Having direction for your daily steps and what you want from life will keep you motivated, engaged and growing.

Your goals might change over time too, and that's okay. They're not written in stone, but don't let them just remain as promises on a paper that you look back on in years with sadness. You might even struggle to come up with five goals, that's normal as well – so just start with one if that's easier. What is your big dream? The one that keeps you awake at night and works as a reminder that you could be doing more with your life?

Lastly, I write five things to be thankful for each day. This list changes depending on where I am and what I am up to. Being in Britain I often feel the need to practise gratitude when the sun decides to make an appearance. Sometimes, though, I am thankful for a lovely message on Instagram from a podcast listener. Other times I might write about someone in my life whom I'm feeling grateful for, or just a random act of kindess that has improved my day.

This ritual sets me up for a great day because it keeps me driven and inspired. It reminds me of my goals and purpose

"Be the change you want to see in the world" was the mantra I kept repeating to myself.

in life, and primes my brain for the activities and actions I am working towards, which is really what it is all about.

From the beginning, I knew that Smart Girl Tribe would be great as a digital magazine to focus on issues that matter: such as mental health, travel, careers and social issues affecting women worldwide. On that first day I wrote the "categories" I wanted to feature on a piece of paper and the first five steps I needed to take. The first stride was to find a web designer, so I emailed my entire contact list hoping someone knew someone who could make a recommendation. And they did, so my first SGT hire was made.

While the website was being developed (which took three months), I set about promoting the venture across social media which at the time was my Twitter account. I contacted budding writers every day to find those wanting to write about topics other than boyfriends and losing weight. On launch day, the website received so many hits that it crashed. As I hit "live" with my website developer I watched the numbers skyrocket. That was an unforgettable day.

I wasn't sure at first where Smart Girl Tribe would go; it was a passion of mine, that I truly felt was needed.

From having the idea, to launching the Smart Girl Tribe magazine and sending out that first email to finding a web designer, only took a couple of hours. I knew I was onto something and that it was an idea to run with. My parents were self-employed and had instilled strong entrepreneurial traits in me, but none of my friends had big ideas about wanting to create a business at that stage. It was a risk, but it was something I knew at my very core that I needed to carry out.

Trust me, millions of people right now are living a life based on someone else's beliefs. Don't let that be you. People will always expect and even command that you conform. If you haven't thought about owning your identity, now is the time to start. Only *you* can control your thoughts, feelings, actions and ultimate destiny. Never allow someone else's definition of happiness or success to determine the course of your life.

Every single morning you wake up you can choose who to live for. It's similar to a Year 4 maths test – everyone has to concentrate on their own paper. Tune out everybody else's opinions – the "white noise" – and listen to your own voice, dreams and ambition. It is only when you silence the others that you find the passion that will awaken you and set your soul on fire.

SMART GIRL ACTIONS

- Work through the Rate Your Passions exercise to help you identify your passions and build time into your life to pursue them.
- Say "yes" to one new thing per week. It could be big or small, but that three-letter word matters most.
- Complete The 5–5–5 Rule exercise and let yourself dream big.
- Each morning, decide to live for you, not for someone else.

CHAPTER 2

I PROMISE TO LEARN HOW TO DEAL WITH THE FEAR OF FAILURE

"I'm going to quit," I tell myself.

It has been 20 days, 14 hours and about 43 minutes.

"They'll all think I'm mad. They'll ask me about my Plan B." I didn't even have a Plan A, so that would just be more stress to endure. I continued to argue with myself.

"What if they laugh? What if they don't 'get it'? What if this is my biggest failing to date?"

Standing in the Corinthia hotel in Central London, to my left the room was full of celebrities and to my right was the paparazzi. And I was going to walk away from it.

This was supposed to be my dream job, organizing events for Louis Vuitton and Tiffany's. I was less than three weeks in and had been given the task of organizing an event for Hollywood stars and the British press. The photographers were asking for poses, the hotel guests were asking for autographs and my boss was already offering me a promotion. "But . . ." That three-letter word was haunting me.

I didn't feel that the job meant enough to *me*. To quote Emily Blunt in *The Devil Wears Prada*, this was a job that "a million girls would kill for", and to think I actually had the audacity to believe the job wasn't serious enough for me, yet I did.

In my heart, I knew that my passion project – Smart Girl Tribe – could be a fully fledged business. So many different people told me during my final year of university that it would never amount to anything. With my grades, I was encouraged to choose a more academic path: lawyer, interpreter and politician were just a handful of the jobs being pushed my way. Professors even called my parents to assure them I was destined for greater things than Smart Girl Tribe, suggesting I apply for a prestigious position at the European Union. Where would I be if I had followed that path, I wonder?

It would be great to tell you that I didn't listen. But I did – to *every* opinion, and I accepted the first reputable, glossy-sounding job offered to me. Two weeks after receiving my cap and gown, I found myself working in this glamorous job in London and was miserable.

Standing in the middle of that sumptuous room surrounded by stars, I was living my life according to what I *should* do. Despite having everything to make me happy

– a great job, living situation and family – in pure 21-year-old fashion, on the train home after the event I played Kelly Clarkson's "Stronger", then quit my job with absolutely no plan about what to do next. Not even half a plan – zero plan.

Fresh out of university I was petrified that I'd never find another job, my parents wouldn't understand and I wouldn't be able to pay my rent. Feeling the fear in every inch of me, I did the only thing I could and surrendered to it. I booked a one-way flight to New York – a dream of mine. You *always* have the choice to rise from the rubble.

The Big Apple was exactly how I'd imagined. This was my Holly Golightly moment, apart from the fact that I had *no* apartment, *no* friends and *no* job. Did I mention I also had absolutely *no* reason to think this was a good idea? New York is remarkable, and there is an electricity about it which you notice as soon as you touch down. The skyscrapers could have been overwhelming and the New Yorkers are a breed apart, but it felt right.

The first thing to secure was a job, and not just any job. I hadn't moved eight hours across the Atlantic for nothing. Putting on my "confident" hat, I booked a meeting with the editor of the second largest political media outlet in the States. What did it take? A call from me every Monday for six weeks, leaving voicemails to assure him I wasn't going to stop until I had a meeting with him.

I knew exactly what I wanted to say and had prepared a portfolio of my *BathImpact* pieces and clippings from Smart Girl Tribe. The editor's room oozed journalistic spirit. There were writers at desks tapping away, a newsroom adjacent to the main room delivering breaking news, and TV screens in each corner to show the latest global happenings. I got the job.

At this stage, SGT was still a digital magazine so I planned to freelance at another publication, honing my journalistic skills. Result. Mornings were spent in a Starbucks working on SGT and my evenings back at the apartment writing for the newspaper.

Did everything happen quickly in New York? Nope. I stayed in a hotel for a couple of weeks then was lucky enough to meet a friend to crash with. We spent hours walking around Central Park, nights on top of the Empire State Building discussing my plans, and mornings devouring coffee at Barnes & Noble. Even Carrie Bradshaw would have been jealous.

It had been a major risk, moving to the big city, and I was making it, leaving behind everything stable and secure. People said I would fail (my second favourite F word after feminism). Was I a failure? I had quit, right? I had "failed" at the esteemed job, given up a steady income and secure future. Given up on the checklist that the world said should matter.

That failure is called Smart Girl Tribe.

EVERYTHING HAPPENS AS IT SHOULD

We all have a life "checklist", and we're not always conscious of it. I'm guilty of one too – of thinking "By the time I'm 30..."

I remember one summer day, in the final year of uni, I was sitting with my two best girlfriends, Emma and Hannah.

"If I'm going to be a lawyer for a big city law firm in London by the time I am 26, I'm going to need to have completed my legal training by 24 and to have set up contacts with potential placements the year before that, so I am going to have to start connecting with lawyers and building my experience now!" Emma shared with us. She did graduate as a lawyer and pursue a position as a solicitor in a top firm in Paris a whole five years later than her life plan dictated, and is now insanely happy.

Go on, admit that you have a "Before I'm 20/30/40" list too. We all do. Who handpicked a number to represent the age when we should have our career sorted or be on the housing ladder? Why do we put so much pressure on completing everything? Aged 30 is still early, just as is 40 and 50, so throw away that list and buckle up for the best years of your life.

If I had made it as a journalist right out of school (my plan back then) then I wouldn't have had the time to build Smart Girl Tribe. There are so many times in my life I have been upset about not getting something, and in hindsight have realized that it was never meant to be mine.

Your life will unfold as it is meant to.

Sometimes you have to wait for the right moment, until *you* are the person you need to be. Even when Smart Girl Tribe was a success, it was years before I contemplated launching a podcast, because at the beginning I knew I didn't have the skills or confidence to do this. Sometimes things must fall into place first, or you need to have gone through experiences or even certain challenges to meet your destiny.

We also often expect our dream job/relationship/holiday to look a certain way, when the reality is different than we anticipated. Pay attention to those feelings. If you secure a prized promotion, university place, acting job or something you have wanted forever, if you start having contradictory feelings about it then maybe it's not right or meant for you. The secret is to listen to how these dreams make you feel in your body, and pay attention to the way you respond to things. How do you feel when diving into something new? Are you sitting up straight and tall, or is your body contracting or tense or feeling weak? Are your energy levels high or low? Does your body feel light or heavy? Societal expectations can push us to get caught up in something that looks so good on paper that we ignore the negative feelings that come with it. Pump the brakes and take some time to figure out the next best step for *you*.

"Failure" is only what you associate that word with.

"Failing" and quitting that job in London and packing a bag for New York helped me hone my journalistic skills and broaden SGT's reach. Not only that, but it allowed me to follow my passion and led to the opportunity to go full-time with my business. It showed me how to make "failure" work for me – to examine what happened and to understand why, to allow me to move forwards and use these life lessons as a positive force.

Often we women don't follow our passion or make big plans because we're fearful. In this chapter I'm going to help you to look into the three things holding you back: the fear of failing, your past and not wanting to stand out. After all, who wants to run scared when you can run free?

"You gain strength, courage and confidence by every experience in which you really look fear in the face."

—Eleanor Roosevelt

FEAR OF FAILURE

If you had one dream and knew it would come true, what would it be? Would it be starting a blog? Or joining a choir? Or moving to the other side of the world to become a yogini? Hold on to that thought, we're going to revisit it soon.

The truth is that anything worthwhile is going to take hard work, hustle, grit, perseverance and some failure.

It's all well and good growing up with pictures of rainbows in our rooms with lines such as "follow your dreams" around them, but reality isn't like that. Know what I mean? Is anyone else bored of those *inspirational* quotes on Pinterest as well? Or the quirky can-do-it-all people on social media posting about how, with a little faith, all can come true?

You owe the world your dream and the best version of you, but all that is on the other side of fear. Like the pot of gold at the end of the rainbow. If you're so scared about the journey and not reaching the gold, then you end up not doing anything at all and you'll definitely never reach the treasure.

The difference between the women living their dreams and those who are not is that the former are committed to failing again and again, until they reach success. The distinction between a winner and a loser is that a winner shows up one more time. Those women are okay with the idea of failing – they wouldn't let the idea of failing tear them down. You too need to be more obsessed with your dream, than the idea that it could fail.

Obviously, a fear of failing is natural, but a lot of us are so afraid that we miss out on a tonne of opportunities. Remember at school when the teacher asked a question and you thought you knew the answer, but you didn't put your hand up in case it was wrong? Then, as soon as you heard the answer, you wish you had put your hand up and been bold with your knowledge and understanding and risked being wrong. In life, if you don't put your hand up or take the risk in putting your idea out there, you'll miss out on reaching greatness.

One way to think about your fear of failing is to turn it on its head. Stay with me here. For example, if you think: *I want to start a blog, but I can't just sit down and start.* Ask yourself: why? *Because it might be really terrible.* What happens then? *I'll feel really embarrassed.* So? *I'll feel really embarrassed.*

Okay, so you're not starting your blog because you're worried about being really embarrassed. Really?

Remember a few pages ago I asked you what your dream was? Well this is it, here it is. Wouldn't it be more embarrassing if you don't follow your dream out of fear? Are you really going to be the old lady in her rocking chair saying, "I could have done this, but I chose not to because I was scared"? That's not what being a smart girl is about at all.

I started the Smart Girl Tribe website with zero writers, and the podcast from my bedroom. I had no money or experience. Being "ready" to start a project or a dream is a lie, the day you feel completely ready doesn't exist. It's similar to having a baby – you can study the books, hire a nanny or listen to all the podcasts but unless you actually have one and throw yourself into the task wholeheartedly, you're never going to fully succeed.

That fear can stop you from doing anything. We are all so obsessed with needing the latest camera to start a YouTube channel or the best microphone to start a podcast, but you don't need any of that. The key to success (and happiness) is in the starting – remember that pot of gold at the end of the rainbow. Author Jodi Picoult says: "You can always edit a bad page. You can't edit a blank page." When I started, I didn't have a beautiful website and my writing wasn't perfect, but I developed those skills over time. You just need to start. Right now. Today. Well, after reading this book.

Once you start, it's easier to accept failure as a massive part of success. Failure is where all the lessons are, and failure is actually sublime as it helps you recognize the areas where you need to learn and evolve. To become the best version of yourself, you need to keep growing and that's only going to come from messing up from time to time, so stop being afraid of failing and start embracing it. Welcome it in.

One way to accept failure is to find a buddy. Talk to a girlfriend, parent, teacher, lecturer or even your partner, and tell them what your big dream is and what you are afraid of. Ask them to remind you every week about your dream. This will hold you accountable and remind you of your dream so often that you'll feel bad if you're not going after it. You'll either find a way or an excuse, so let's find a way and be determined to smash our goals.

You grow through what you go through.

Talking to someone close to you about your plans means they are totally going to get on board with your ideas. They will ask you what the next step is – which will encourage you to climb up the escalator towards your dream. If you don't have anyone you want to talk to about your goals, or if you are more an introvert than extrovert, then a great investment of mine has been a stick-on whiteboard. I have one in my office so every week I can remind myself what my goals are. Keep working on your 5-5-5 Rule too.

YOUR PAST

What else could hold you back? I hate to tap you on the shoulder and be the ghost of Christmas past, but that's a huge part of your decision to get going and move forwards: your past. As much as I would love a candyfloss world, life doesn't work like that. We are all at some point going to go through challenges. If you've experienced difficulties already, then thank you for reading this book, for your bravery, and for dedicating yourself to leading a better life.

Sometimes we go through such terrible things it makes us want to settle for poor and unhealthy relationships, or it makes us not want to work hard or give our best. You don't need to settle though. I'm here to remind you that you deserve more. You do. You are made for more.

Holding on to the past is similar to carrying around four extra luggage bags. They're heavy, ugly and full of irrelevant history. Put that bag down. Seriously. In the words of Taylor Swift: "Shake it off". You don't need it weighing you down.

If you've gone through something traumatic or turbulent then you know how to survive. Many people live in fear because they don't know what they can handle, but you do. If you have experienced trauma or something that has changed how you see the world, own it and use it. Put all that energy into your dream.

Being a victim and moaning about your situation is a cop-out. Don't indulge in powerless feelings or helpless emotions. Even if you have nothing, truly nothing, you can always change your attitude. Victimizing yourself is the fastest route to taking all the fun out of life. You can't see the magic in the world through victim goggles. Of course, I am not referring to those who have suffered abuse, whether that be mental, emotional or physical. I am deeply sorry if you have gone through any kind of trauma and please know that at Smart Girl Tribe, you are seen, heard and loved.

One of the simplest ways to let go of your past is to forgive. Fear, anger or hatred from our past stops us in our tracks and pulls us away from living the life we are destined to. By holding on to that anger, shame or fear, you poison yourself with those unhelpful negative feelings. You might need to forgive someone who has hurt you, perhaps even a friend or family member. Sometimes it can be a bully you need to forgive or someone who broke up with you. You might also need to forgive *yourself* – maybe you've made a mistake or done something stupid in the past. Have you ever found yourself lying awake at night and your brain reminds you of that stupid mistake you made at 17? Or 25? Or 30? Me too. By not forgiving you are letting the baddies win. Let go of the shame and allow yourself to be human, which means accepting the moments you were "less than" and moving on.

Shame pops up when we least expect it. Lecturer and author Brené Brown explains: "It's the intensely painful feeling that we are unworthy of love and belonging." Sometimes shame is similar to a tidal wave, ready to drown us, and at other times shame is a specific moment we wish we couldn't recall or remember. Maybe you said something you'd rather forget, or hurt someone in a moment. Maybe you spent time in a dark place and you are still holding on to the shame caused. The truth is, you are only as free as are your secrets. If you don't talk about those moments, or at least write them down, then shame will grow inside you, and will invade every fragment of your life. You may have done things you're not proud of, but whatever past memory or mistake you are holding on to, let it go.

Shame also damages us when our social media platforms show the best and hide the rest. You might be feeling less worthy than others because you look up to celebrities or those with fame, success or wealth, forgetting that celebrities feel just as you do sometimes. Letting regret fester in your mind will torture you.

EXERCISE: FIND YOUR EXPERIENCE

Everyone says that our friends can relate to us – but sometimes that's not true. When I was younger my best friend Emily became very close to another girl in our class. I couldn't understand how they had become close so quickly and in such a short amount of time. Emily explained to me that her new friend was the only other girl in our year who knew what it felt like to have her parents divorce, and that was a powerful bond.

If you cannot find anyone around you who relates to your past experience or trauma then look for them. Your story will have been told before, you just need to find that person or people. Track down old friends, support groups, try social media hashtags or head to the autobiography section at a store to find a story that discusses how it felt and how someone else coped with a similar experience.

Some of us go through a bunch of battles – not the endearing kind but the tough ones that stay with us for the rest of our lives. Life is tricky, but you are deserving of a beautiful life that isn't defined by suffering, and you are only going to be able to give that to yourself if you set yourself free. See your past situations as a cage and you as the bird. You own that key now.

STAND OUT, SISTER

Do you try to avoid standing out? Have you ever worried about seeming different? Don't most people feel more comfortable fitting in? Heck, yes.

Especially women.

When we want to stand out, we hear this little voice in our heads reminding us of all our little flaws and imperfections, and the risk involved in being different, of trying something new. Even when we muster up the courage to stand up and stand out, we're often tempted to sit right back down again.

Most of the time we don't want to stand out because we're paranoid about what others will think and say. You know when a celebrity wears a particular colour or designer, suddenly everyone wants it? Well, girl-world is a little like that. We all grew up with the most popular girl in the club or class influencing what people wore or how they talked, or setting the new trend. But why fit in and follow the crowd when you were born to stand out?

What other people think of you is none of your business. You know all of those films where there's the heroine and her friend, right? Well, when you choose to not stand up and not stand out, you're just settling for playing "the friend". And you are worth more.

I get that it's hard – this dilemma of standing out while wanting to fit in at the same time. Remember that girl in the movie who was always in the library? (Nope. Because nobody does.) That was me in school. Was I called out for it? Absolutely. Ignoring the name calling, in whatever form, was my way of standing out. I was actually proud when people started calling me Granger (after the one-and-only Hermione), and I loved that I had clubs after school that were so much fun that I didn't have time to worry about boys or mean girls.

Yes, of course the struggle for identity and working out who you are is taxing. You'd like to be different but also want to be one of the crowd – we all want to be accepted and valued. Here is the truth: you can be an extrovert, an introvert, loud or quiet, bookish or wild, and yet not want to stand out. You have got to be okay with being yourself and not agonize about conventionally "fitting in".

Choose to stand out in different ways. It might be through your own personal style, or sharing what you believe in.

Perhaps you are super-athletic, or a library girl like me. All these ways of living are good. No, they're great. If you have a nose ring or pink hair, rock them. If you love going to Cosplay conventions, be proud of it.

We all think way too much about what people think of us, when actually, nobody cares. Most people are busy worrying about their own lives instead of noticing yours. Sharing your real self will show you how you're not judged for it, but that your distinction is something people want to embrace and understand. Take the first step, and every step after that will seem easier. Start by striking up one conversation about something that really matters to you – an interest or a passion – or something that isn't well known about your life. It is a way of pushing yourself out of your comfort zone, and will bring others closer to you when they learn what matters to you.

I have had the opportunity to work with some incredible trailblazers, including the TED speaker Laura Young. Laura is an advocate for climate change and captured my attention when she noticed how much plastic she was throwing away, literally. Laura started sharing her realization with her family and friends, encouraging them to change and live plastic-free. Laura became a TED speaker and her blog advocating for climate change has impacted thousands of lives. Imagine if Laura had never shared her passion and story, out of fear or

Nobody has the right to tell you who to be, and the sooner you learn and love who you are, the easier it will be.

worry. This is the ripple effect one person owning their values and mission can have.

Consider the story of Ramla Ali, the boxer, who also shows how important it is to own your differences. She says: "When I was younger, I was always concerned with how people perceived me. It's the reason I walked into a boxing gym in the first place." That gym was in her adoptive home of Bethnal Green, East London, where Ali moved with her family as a toddler to escape the ravages of the Somali Civil War in the early 1990s. Like many refugees, she is unsure of her exact birthday or age, and for many years had to hide her boxing career from her parents for fear of it bringing shame on the family. She is now the most decorated female Muslim boxer in history and won her first UK national title in 2016.

UpCircle Beauty's founder Anna Brightman created an entire line of organic and sustainable beauty products from waste coffee grounds. UpCircle Beauty has been wildly successful but wouldn't have been if Anna hadn't stood up for what she believed in. You can check out her interview with me on the Smart Girl Tribe podcast, along with Laura's.

Perhaps you're thinking, "Okay, Scarlett, you were brave and valiant enough to stand out, but how can I?" You, sister, are allowed to be it all. Too often we try fitting into one box when the truth is we can be everything we want to be.

Start now by reframing "failure" – and welcoming it as part of your future, something you will experience as you pursue your dreams, a natural part of the growing and learning process.

If we understand that, we gain the freedom to stand up for who we are and what we dream of. Why not start with that one conversation, even if it's with me? Honestly – message me on socials and let me know what you are loving at the moment and what makes you beautifully you, I would *love* to hear. Connect with other readers of this book in our Facebook group – the Smart Girl Tribe Society.

SMART GIRL ACTIONS

- Use the Find Your Experience exercise to learn about others who have shared your history and overcome it.
- You could write a letter to forgive either yourself or others who have hurt you. This will get your thoughts out of your own head, you will be able to see on paper the incidents, mistakes or regrets you are still holding on to. If writing your letter to yourself, write it with love, compassion and understanding.
- Start a conversation about something distinctive about your life or interests. Choose a friend, maybe someone you have just met, and tell them one thing about yourself that makes you unique and different from many other people. Maybe you like a particular TV show that lots of your friends can't connect with. Or it could just be the reasons why you choose to wear dungarees or why you want to travel to Thailand or Japan. Sharing your personality in this way helps you to stand out and own who you are.

CHAPTER 3

I PROMISE TO LEARN TO COPE WITH ANXIETY AND START SPEAKING MY TRUTH

Close to death experiences might include crashing a motorbike or being in a car crash on a first date (both of which I have gone through, and no I didn't see him again.). This was different though. I was 15 years old and in a local music store, trying to distract myself from what had happened earlier that morning when my parents had told me we would be moving to a new country, again.

I was sweating in places I didn't think were possible. My throat was dry, my heart was pounding and my eyes wouldn't focus. Was I about to faint? Or collapse? What was happening to me?

An elderly woman standing nearby asked if I was okay. Was I? I didn't even know. Looking into her eyes, I couldn't say anything.

No one had heard of the term panic attack really back then, which is what was happening to me, just as nobody talked about "anxiety". Even then, though, I knew that this meant a rough journey ahead.

When we are young we are told to make sure we exercise and eat healthily; we are lectured about how necessary it is for our physical health. Yet we don't give the same amount of importance to our mental health – why?

At school or university, even in the workplace, it is common to face anxiety or overwhelming feelings of stress from exam pressure, friendship group problems or social life challenges. Anxiety is a term we throw around lightly, but the World Health Organization says, "1 in 3 people around the world suffer from anxiety" ... so many of us do or will suffer with it. Some of you will know how frightening it feels to be drowning in a panic attack.

If I look back over my life, I can see when my anxiety first developed. I first started having panic attacks around the time I moved back to the UK from Italy. I felt different from my peers. Dealing with bullies and the worry about "being too different" manifested itself as panic attacks. For some, small triggers spark the attacks, for others they are the result of big decisions or ongoing stress. Even if you are able to address the fundamental reason why you are anxious, often

Our brains deserve just as much attention as the rest of our body.

you will have to learn to manage an ongoing relationship with your mental health.

In those times when I have been more prone to feeling anxious, I have needed to explore additional and creative ways to help me cope, ideas that I hope sharing with you will be helpful. Trust me, if Amanda Seyfried, Emma Stone and Janet Jackson can be open about their mental health struggles and realize there's no shame in it, so can you.

I want to encourage you to start taking your mental health seriously.

WHY DOES ANXIETY HAPPEN?

Anxiety happens when our body kicks into "fight or flight" mode. What does that mean? Our bodies are set up to either run from an issue or deal with it, and when your body thinks it's in danger, anxiety kicks in.

I like to imagine that everyone has a car alarm inside them. For some it will go off at just a gust of wind, while others' alarms only go off when a window is smashed or the car is completely broken into. Anxiety is actually your nervous system trying to protect you from the dangers your brain perceives around you, and for some of us that anxiety alert is more sensitive than others.

Anxiety makes life difficult when it holds you back from doing the things you really want to do, and leaves you feeling mentally and physically drained. Realizing that this can happen again and again can even stop you doing things for fear that you might have an anxiety attack.

According to Klaus Bernhardt in his book *The Anxiety Cure: Live a Life Free From Panic In Just a Few Weeks*, on the subject of dealing with worry, stress and panic, "you shouldn't be trying to fight your feelings of panic but instead work at resisting them." Here are some favourite methods of mine to stave off the panic and protect your mental health.

EXERCISE: THE 5-SENSE RULE

Some tools have hugely helped my anxiety. The most effective for me has been the 5-Sense Rule. Whenever I feel myself starting to get panicked or worried, I concentrate on my senses: sight, hearing, smell, taste and touch. As a society we focus on what to do once a panic attack is happening, but I find it more beneficial to work to prevent and temper my anxiety or anxious feelings as soon as they begin.

When feeling particularly stressed or overwhelmed, ask yourself: what can I see? What can I hear? What can I smell? What can I taste? And what can I touch? By focusing on my senses in the present moment I distract myself from the trigger for my anxiety. You might be able to hear birds or cars passing. Maybe you can feel the necklace around your neck or feet in your shoes. What can you see? Really centre on what is all around you. Can you taste or smell anything? This practice is a fantastic tool to ground you and your thoughts wherever you are, one that will stop your mind from spinning out of control and calm you down.

I have known Smart Girl Tribe team members to use this method on the tube, on a busy high street while shopping, and even at music festivals. It genuinely is a technique that can be used anywhere.

KNOW YOUR TRIGGERS

It's important to be aware of the usual events or situations that you struggle with. Timing is a common concern for me and many others. As with the 5-Sense exercise, my aim is to try to avoid letting my anxiety take over so I have learned not to tie myself to fixed times if possible. Setting specific times can maximize stress so go at your own pace. If you are supposed to meet someone at 12.45, then tell them you will be there between 12.45 and 1pm. This is a very simple method to avoid pressures in everyday life.

Step outside of places and situations where you feel most anxious. Shopping centres used to make me really nervous – it was the thought of so many people all in one place. Now I do my shopping online, or if I need to go somewhere busy then I visit early and leave before or after everyone else. If school, university or work – or somewhere you have to go – makes you anxious then speak with someone in an authoritative position and explain how you feel. There will usually be a pastoral care team or HR who will understand your concerns and will have options they can implement to help with your anxiety.

Often the reason for your feelings will be obvious, but occasionally the trigger is not so clear. Keep a notepad with you and when you start to feel anxious, as hard as it may seem, get out the notepad and pen and try to identify what emotion, person or event is making you feel apprehensive. Sometimes I can feel so anxious that even my anxieties have anxieties, so I can completely relate to how tough this activity might seem.

If it takes time to dig down into the reasons behind your panic moments, don't worry. For instance, my nervousness about busy places comes from the idea of so many people all together in one space. Identifying your triggers helps you to understand and plan so you can work around your anxieties – making it less likely for you to struggle, and also giving you a greater control over your feelings, which is a comfort in itself.

Go through your notepad every so often and see if you notice recurring places or people that cause distress – looking for patterns will guide you to understand your internal protection systems more deeply.

FIND YOUR PERSONAL TONIC

Let's get real for a second: you are going to be fighting anxiety and stress on the offence for the rest of your life. Similar to a football game, if you want to tackle it before it gets up close to you then you need a great defender on the job. A physical activity "stress defender" is a great way to mitigate levels of tension, and improve mood and sleep. You might choose dancing, stretching, or even yoga – it will depend on the body movement or activities that appeal most to you.

A huge help for me is listening to relaxing sounds on my phone and meditation. Have a playlist of soft music and tunes that calm you down. The Calm app is a great tool, it has set meditation moods and sessions easily available to you. The HeadSpace app is also particularly helpful.

When I start feeling stressed, or am about to enter an unavoidable stressful situation, I listen for a few minutes and follow the relaxation practices. Calming sounds and music are a fantastic stress reliever but they don't work for everyone.

There are only so many waves and birds you can hear before you start feeling as though you are lost in a forest of your own creation.

We have a fantastic series of meditations to accompany this book at smartgirltribe.com. For each chapter there is a meditation that will help ease your stress or anxiety and help catapult you into success and being the woman you are destined to be. The meditation for this chapter has been especially designed with you in mind, so you can get a handle on your anxiety.

EXERCISE: ANXIETY-PROOF YOUR WEEK

In the same way that you should watch your schedule for repeating occasions that cause your anxiety to spike, you can also look ahead for ways to avoid problematic times and transitions.

Open up your calendar. Scan and underline the activities that recur every week and prioritize these. Imagine the hours of your day or week as a pie chart: ask yourself what you want to give slices to and what you don't, what makes you feel good and what causes tension. Look for clashes and busy periods that will naturally be more stressful, times that you can foresee will be more difficult.

How does your week balance? There are obviously 24 hours in a day and a whopping 168 hours in a week. If you take out an optimal 8 hours each day for sleep, that still leaves 112 hours of time awake each week. Rejig your pie chart to help your anxiety.

If driving to work gives you anxiety, then work out how long it would take to walk. If your daily post-work call from your mother or friend makes you stressed, then tell her you will speak to her a little later when you're bound to be more relaxed, maybe with your feet up and a glass of wine in hand.

Large and small tweaks to your daily and weekly habits can really change your moods and anxiety levels and help you bring your life back under control.

Crystal healer Steff Pitman recommends pretending you are putting on an invisible cloak for protection in a stressful situation. Imagine putting on your cloak to shield yourself from the negative energy coming your way. Steff also suggests burning sage when coming home after a bad day. White sage is said to release negative ions and neutralize positive ions so this could clear the air. Choosing to let go of negative thoughts in a ritual like this sets your intention and dedication to self-improvement and can be the beginning of your change in mindset.

RECLAIM YOUR SPACE

Cultivate a calming space in your home. In a corner, set up a candle and mood lighting so you have somewhere to go to calm your mood when you need. Create a space that aligns with how you want to feel; your subconscious mind is scanning and processing your environment all the time so make sure your immediate surroundings are clear from any clutter, and help you feel safe and supported.

According to Smart Girl Tribe contributor Becky Stanton: "The Feng Shui technique called the Power Position means you choose the space within a room where you feel most powerful and in command. Usually, it's a spot where you can see all entrances and there is a solid wall behind you. You can head there after a stressful moment to feel empowered again."

EXERCISE: "LET GO" PRACTICE

Anxiety can creep up on you, at least it does for me. I can be in a queue and suddenly my frustration about how long it is taking will turn into anxiety, or I receive an unexpected email that rubs me up the wrong way and my annoyance builds up and that manifests an hour or two later in anxious feelings.

We constantly lose focus and control of our emotional energy as we transition and race between activities.

As you move from one action to another, close your eyes and repeat the words "let go" several times. This allows us to release any stress we are holding on to, and then we can enter a new activity with an open mind and positive mindset.

If I am about to take on a mighty task, I might even set up an alarm every 50 minutes on my phone, a reminder to let go of any negative feelings I have, that stops the anxious ones building up. Why 50 minutes? Because according to research, 50 minutes is the length of time for which most people can direct their attention.

GRATEFUL THANKS

You know how there is a corrective for everything? An opposing force? Well, the opposite of anxiety is gratitude. Probably not according to the dictionary, but it is according to the Smart Girl Tribe rules.

I often tell the Smart Girl Tribe audience that anxiety and gratitude are two emotions you *cannot* feel simultaneously. Neuroscientist and author Alex Korb explains in *The Grateful Brain*: "Gratitude can have such a powerful impact on your life because it engages your brain in a virtuous cycle. Your brain only has so much power to focus its attention. It cannot easily focus on both positive and negative stimuli so you literally can't be grateful and anxious at the same time."

Gratitude isn't the same as happiness either, gratitude resonates deeper. Most of us are happy when something great happens – if we receive a gift or the jumper we have been after for months is discounted for instance. Gratitude, though, isn't dependent on specific events, and is "impervious to change," says Janice Kaplan, author of *The Gratitude Diaries*: "Gratitude requires an active emotional involvement, you can't be passively grateful, you have to stop and feel it, experience the emotion so it creates an inner richness that's sustaining in difficult times as well as good ones."

If you struggle to practise gratitude then try the 5-5-5 rule I mentioned in Chapter One. This definitely holds me accountable every day.

Soon enough, gratitude will become a habit, and the more you look for things to be grateful for, the more you find – even when your colleague is driving you crazy or work isn't going your way.

If you can manage to be grateful for what you have, and give yourself time to meditate on all of your blessings, your anxiety won't be able to win.

I didn't write this book for your partner, teachers or boss but *you*, because I want to share the actions you can take today to transform the common problems and issues you face. Anxiety

You are never too young or old to live in gratitude for what is around you and the simple pleasures of life.

doesn't mean you're not good enough or not smart enough, it just means you have to work on your habits. Decide that you won't let your past be your future.

Being a writer, I naturally love writing letters. When I first started having panic attacks I would write a letter to myself later that day to reassure me that I was okay afterwards, and to know in the future that everything is fine. I keep hold of those letters for the next time, and when I start to feel stressed or worried I look back at them, as if I am having a conversation with my future self which helps to calm me down. To make sure my letters are accessible I keep them in my bedside table. I use my 5-Sense Rule when I am out and feeling panicked, but the letters I read when at home and I'm feeling my anxiety rising.

THAT INNER VOICE

Anxiety can also originate from our self-limiting beliefs, your inner mean girl telling you that you can't do something (more on that later). These beliefs often stem from fear – of rejection, of people laughing at us, of being wrong or failing, or of not being good enough. They stop us from doing or saying or acting in the way we want to. At events, I love getting the audience engaged and involved. Often, I will ask everyone – *everyone* – to think of their dream. Then I ask someone to share theirs with the group and there is silence. Seriously – I can hear crickets, it's that quiet. I know everyone has thought of something, so why doesn't anyone have the confidence to share?

I joke that people are slumping down in their seats, reluctant to stand up because they're thinking about their boy-/girlfriend or they are slowly falling asleep, or perhaps they're busy planning their grocery list. It's actually those limiting beliefs that are stopping them, the assumptions that hold you back and stop you from pushing for and achieving what you are capable of. They live in our subconscious mind and as over 90 per cent of our actions arise from our subconscious, these false beliefs play a huge role in nearly everything we do.

If you have an audacious goal, or any kind of objective for that matter, or if you want to be successful, you need to programme your mind to erase that inner critic within you saying that you're not enough, you can't do it or will fall flat on your face. Every time you catch yourself telling yourself something nasty or horrible, you have the power to take control of your thoughts. Replace the negative thoughts with empowering messages that will help you towards your goal. Rather than believe that you "can't do it", start telling yourself that you *can*, and *will*.

IN IT TOGETHER

You might not suffer with anxiety – I sincerely hope you don't – but it can sometimes be just as tough to watch someone else go through it. If you are with someone in the middle of a panic attack, the best way to look after them is to make sure they are safe and to reassure them.

Make them aware that you are there with them and that there's no pressure for them to do anything. Tell them to breathe in for four, hold it for four and breathe out for four. Remind them that nothing bad is going to come from this, that everything will be okay and ask them to concentrate on you. When going through a panic attack, it can be hard to focus on anything, and instead you get swept up in the whirlwind that it is, so keep telling them to concentrate on their breathing and the words you are saying. Call for extra help and support if needed.

There are so many ways you can support a friend with anxiety. When someone talks about themselves negatively, give them positive feedback and show that you care about them and their wellbeing. Create a happy playlist full of songs telling them how powerful and unique they are and share it with them.

As the award-winning documentary maker Elena Mannes discusses in her book *The Power of Music*, "scientists have found that music stimulates more parts of the brain than any other human function". When people are struggling they tend to spend a lot of time alone so this is the perfect way to lift them up - it's something they can enjoy in a quiet moment when they're sad, on their morning walks or on their way to work.

Starting a new hobby or class together is another effective way to distract someone who is struggling. It doesn't have to be an exercise class – it could be a craft or language class you can enjoy together. Having a regular commitment is something your friend can look forward to each week. I once committed to a "Year of Fun" with a friend. Each month I would take him to do something different, which helped him refocus and have something to be regularly excited about and look forward to. We went rollerblading and ice skating, we attended a pottery class and even tried a Chinese calligraphy class together.

When someone feels under pressure, they are often concerned about being judged or seeming silly. Opening yourself up to this person will help them to trust you in the future and share when they're going through a challenging time. If you can't relate or are worried about doing or saying the wrong thing, borrow a book from the library or research online to educate yourself further, before taking that next step. There are also mental health charities and helplines that are hugely informative and supportive – see the Resources at the back of the book for more information.

Anxiety can be a challenging issue to face, especially if you don't have a strong network around you. Accepting that anxiety will be part of your life is the first step toward easing it, the second is knowing that the future is always brighter after a panic attack. No matter where you are and who you are, remember that you are not alone in this.

SMART GIRL ACTIONS

- Practice the 5-Senses Rule until it is your natural response to rising stress levels.
- Anxiety-proof your week to find ways to delete avoidable stresses from your life.
- Try the "Let Go" exercise, or use a similar mantra to work through moments of anxiety.
- Head to smartgirltribe.com and download the meditations that accompany this book. There is one for each chapter and our "anxiety" meditation has been exclusively designed with you in mind.
- Write a letter from your future self. It can be difficult when living in the present moment to remind ourselves to be calm. The 5-Sense Rule has sometimes proven hard to act on when I'm on the brink of a panic attack.
- Share, open up just like a piñata – we are all stronger together when we find the strength to show our vulnerabilities and fears.

CHAPTER 4

I PROMISE TO SLAY THE MEAN GIRLS AND BUILD A STRONG TRIBE OF TRUE FRIENDS

When name-called and bullied for the first time, I was eight years old. It was my teacher who advised my parents that I transfer schools. Little did I know that less than a decade later I would be faced with bullies a lot scarier than eight-year-olds – faceless internet trolls.

A troll used to be just one of those odd dolls with neon-coloured hair, then the internet changed that. Setting up a business and having an online platform provides a lot of prestigious opportunities, but one not-so-glamorous aspect of going out on your own is online bullying, or trolling. The first few years that I was building the business, I only received positive feedback and responses. However, as soon as Smart Girl Tribe began gaining significant traction and I was becoming recognized, along came the trolls.

On my birthday, a couple of years after university, I was abroad with my family and having a superb time over pizza (you can take the girl out of Italy but seemingly, not Italy out of the girl) when a notification appeared on my screen. It was an Instagram DM – a string of insults about my appearance and the way I spoke. Even though it was my birthday and I was on a huge natural high, my mood plummeted with a large thud. I wanted to think this was another faceless internet troll trying to take down the ambitious, but no. This troll had a name, a name I was familiar with. This girl messaging me had been in the same class as me at secondary school, and it had been four years since I had last seen her.

Even as CEO and Founder of the UK's number one female empowerment organization, I was never given a superhero cape that made me exempt from daily issues and struggles. I have had plenty of experience with mean girls. From moving school to avoid them at eight, to battling spiteful comments throughout my teenage years. Trust me, whether on social media or school halls, I have seen and heard it all. If anyone can take on the inner workings of mean girls, it's me.

The Instagram DM that arrived on my birthday stuck with me for days afterwards. Was she right? Heck, no. But I wasn't going to let her win by getting upset, especially in front of my family. Instead, I replied with kindness. Yes, you read that right. I genuinely felt sorry for her that she had nothing better to do

As soon as you hear or read someone else's words about you, you get to decide whether you will give those words power or not.

than to come up with a nasty comment and actually send it to me, someone she hadn't seen in years. Women can find ways to jab pain hard and deep; I actively decide to rise above the fray and move on with grace and dignity.

MEAN GIRLS

When we are young, we are told that girls are mean because they are *jealous*. No matter how many times I was told that, though, it never made me feel better; it only made me want to crawl into a ball and have the ground swallow me whole. Now I can appreciate the truth in this. Come close and listen up: other people's opinions about you are simply a reflection of their own insecurities. This girl being ghastly to me actually had nothing to do with my reality. I could look different and sound different but even then she would find another way to try to tear me down to make herself feel better. The same was true for all of the mean girls during my teen years and mean women I have encountered since.

When a bully says something hateful, you know that they're trying to provoke a reaction from you – trying to say something to hurt you. Girl-on-girl cruelty is the worst. Women understand women, so they know deep down what will hurt another woman. They use gossip and social exclusion to target your weak spots and hit you where it hurts most.

"The moment anyone tries to demean or degrade you in any way, you have to know how great you are. Nobody would beat you down if you were not a threat," says the actress and former fashion model, Cicely Tyson.

Don't look at the female being mean to you as an "enemy" – try to understand where she is coming from. Often a girl is mean because she feels threatened. Don't stoop to her level and, instead, think about why she is doing it. Turn your attention from the words or content to the motivation behind the words. Do these mean girls say similar things to other people? Is this part of their treatment of people they don't connect with? What is it about you that they have a problem with? As soon as you disassociate yourself from the content of what they say to look at the issues behind their behaviour, it becomes easier to detach yourself from the words. You always deserve to be treated with kindness and respect, so don't settle for anything less.

I have frequently been called *too* everything: "too ambitious", "too focused", "too meticulous" as well as "too different", a "nerd" and a "geek". These are all names I wear proudly – which I admit is much easier to say now, in hindsight. If I'd given up all those years ago when bullies targeted me though, I wouldn't be where I am now. Being "too" focused has led me to the Houses of Parliament, attending events with Emma Watson and being invited to deliver a talk

You are you and that is *your* superpower.

at Harvard University. Being such a "nerd" and an avid reader has meant that when meeting some of the smartest people in the world, I have been able to hold my own and stand tall.

It will never be your life experiences that define who you are, but how you react and handle each situation, and what you take from it. Use each experience to grow, heal and expand your life. There will be days when it's hard to fully commit to being the best version of yourself and the name calling gets to you. Embrace every emotion. Remember in *Gilmore Girls* when Dean breaks up with Rory and Lorelai has to remind her that it's okay to wallow? Life is the same. Try to be the sunniest version of yourself, but accept that you need to sit in the stillness when you're not feeling so sunny. We all need some darkness to appreciate the light.

> *"Hurt people hurt people, that's how pain patterns get passed on, generation after generation, break the chain today, meet anger with sympathy, contempt with compassion, cruelty with kindness. Greet grimaces with smiles. Forgive and forget about finding fault. Love is the weapon of the future."*
>
> — **Yehuda Berg**

As much as I could sit here saying how life-changing it would be to all just be considerate of each other's feelings, I know that won't help you when coming across a mean girl. Their often subtle and insidious forms of behaviour are harder to deflect from or rise above, which is why working on your self-worth is a key part of building healthy relationships.

Sometimes even your friends can be mean girls, and no doubt each of us will have had mean girl moments – times when we've spoken against another female because we're envious, angry, struggling or whatever. Whether you've been one or are dealing with one, I have compiled a list of the different types of mean girls out there and what to do when approached or attacked. Let's be honest, they can be found at the school gates or in your office. Is it a surprise that 55% of adults report being bullied at some point during their adult lives? Those who are bullies in childhood often continue this behaviour as adults, they tend to become more furtive and sly as they age, and their bullying increasingly subtle and hard to expose. However and wherever it happens, bullying is out of order at any age. To help you rise above their behaviours, these are the main types of bullies you will likely meet in life.

THE ENVIOUS MEAN GIRL

Many mean girls want what other girls and women have. Somehow we have a natural tendency to automatically think that the woman next to us is better. This might be about looks, clothes, grades or securing a promotion, but the envious mean girl will go to great lengths to hurt someone they are jealous of, someone whose strengths feed the bully's own insecurities. They might spread rumours about her, or use any influence they have to counteract what she has and "bring her down". For example, if a girl has great grades then the mean girl might call her stupid or imply that she has cheated, or if you win a promotion over a mean girl, then she will try to undermine your new position professionally.

THE POWER-GRABBING MEAN GIRL

Ambition isn't a dirty word. However, there are some mean girls for whom the most important thing is how others see them – from what car they drive to who they are dating and how they dress. Beware of these mean girls for they won't let anyone get in their way. If they see you as competition or a potential obstacle to their own rise, then you are going to have to deal with them to avoid them becoming a major pain in your life. They can also come disguised in the form of a harmful frenemy– they will try and be your friend but purely because you might be useful for their reputation or kudos.

THE CLIQUE MEAN GIRL
Just like vampires need blood, mean girls feed off other mean girls, so they usually hang around their own kind. Even if a girl doesn't seem unkind, if she is hanging around other mean girls then be wary – usually there are unspoken rules about being in this particular clique and it's not one you want to be a part of. Don't sacrifice who you are or who you are destined to be. The mean girl group will often look shiny and popular from the outside, but they are just as unkind to each other on the inside. That's drama you just don't need in your life.

RISING ABOVE IT
Mean girls can happen to you whatever your religion, ethnicity or age and nobody deserves to be treated badly or made to feel inferior. You have amazing positive traits to offer

the world, and need to remember that the problem isn't with you – it is with them.

Simply smiling and remaining confident in who you are is one of the quickest ways to defuse their power, because mean girls get bored. Simple habits such as good posture, a strong speaking voice and making eye contact are all actions that deter mean girls; they are, after all, looking for an easy target.

I can't say their comments won't get to you because the truth is you will find yourself having to live and work with them, even after high school (they're usually the ones who didn't grow up) but remaining strong in your own self-worth is the simplest barrier to their words.

> *"Love is louder, we can respond in kindness because the people who are bullying you, they're insecure about who they are, and that's why they're bullying you. It never has to do with the person they're bullying. They desperately want to be loved and be accepted and they go out of their way to make people feel unaccepted so that they're not alone."*

> **— Madelaine Petsch**

TAKE ACTION

Now that we live in a digital world and 3.8 billion people are on social media, comments can be seen by hundreds and sometimes thousands of people and online bullying is out of control. It's even more imperative that we learn how to keep these bullies in their place and out of our heads. Here are the ways in which you can react positively and proactively if you are being bullied, picked on or targeted by a mean girl – whatever your age.

CONFRONT

When someone knows they can treat you badly, they will continue the same behaviour, so being mentally prepared to have this conversation will help you in the long run. Prepare in advance what you would like to say. On the day you want to have the conversation, choose an outfit that makes you feel empowered and strong, and consider inviting a friend along with you for moral support. Nip the behaviour in the bud and have the conversation early in the bullying situation in order to take control. If this leads to more serious actions, then move to the next stage and report it.

SPEAK UP

If you feel seriously threatened, report it to someone in a position of power or authority, even if this is your boss. You can't let it fester. There are processes in place to help you navigate what you should do. Blocking and reporting is nothing to be afraid of.

Sometimes the best way to avoid a conflict spiralling is to talk to someone you are close with. It might just be opening up to your mum. Hiding your anxiety – for example, about going to work because of bullies – will make your professional life a lot harder. Work is one place everyone should feel accepted and safe. If you find yourself in a bitchy office environment, either choose to rise above it or report it to HR. It's the reason they're there.

EXERCISE: WHO IS YOUR NEMESIS?

As I've already discussed, one way to take the sting out of the words of the bully is to try to understand where she is coming from.

Perhaps the person being mean to you is having a tough time at home and is taking it out on you because they see you have a loving family. Perhaps they can see your inner strengths and wish they had that steel too. It could be as simple as you being there when they were

---

feeling bad and they wanted to take it out on someone, or they had a need to draw attention to themselves by picking on someone else.

Once you look past their words and give meaning to the reason they might have to come out with unnecessary vitriol, you move past being the victim and take control of the situation. Rise up.

IF YOUR FRIEND IS THE BULLY

Sometimes, it's your frenemy whose behaviour you need to decide how to deal with. This is both a more complex and a simpler situation to tackle. Maybe the meanest girl of them all is your closest friend, and trust me – that's not a friendship you need. You shouldn't have to deal with unkind behaviour from those close to you, but you are in the best position to understand why things might not be working in the friendship. You could:

LOCK IN OR LOCK OUT

Ask yourself what you want from this friendship and why it is important. We all want to feel accepted and embraced, so figure out what you are looking for and then apply that to the people who want you to be their friend.

There were only so many times I could go on being "too ambitious" before I realized that I had a choice: to either listen to what I was being told, or to myself and what *I* believed to be true. Why is it easier to believe negative comments over positive statements? Maybe you're reading this having said something horrible about someone else, even a friend. There are no excuses. Everyone knows how hard mean comments can be, and gossip is just a cheap way to try to get attention. Girl-world is always stronger when we are working together.

Competitiveness between girls is a behaviour that is hurting us, and it doesn't need to. I don't buy in to the idea that women have to be backstabbing or catty to get ahead; the future can only be bright for girls if we all collectively realize we are actually playing on the same team – that no woman is above or below us.

CHOOSE "CHARACTER" INSTEAD
If you want your friends to be kind and trustworthy – and you should – then don't settle for less. Having a friend who is *sometimes* nice doesn't make up for a truly good friend either. Cultivate healthy friendships that you know will be part of your life for a long time – is this really the woman you want to be with at your wedding or graduation, or when you're feeling blue? If she isn't delivering what you need, step back before it's too late.

It's never too late to find the friends who are worthy of you.

Everyone at some point feels like an outsider, either someone who has never been asked to prom or a school dance, or missed out on the party invite or doesn't have that group of friends like the ones in films. You might even feel excluded in the office. Anyone else remember when Rachel Green started smoking in *Friends* just to fit in with her colleagues? It's not always easy and it could take time, but keep pushing yourself to get out there and find the friends who don't just validate you but who stretch you and encourage you to go after all of your dreams.

OUR TRIBE

Growing up in the 2000s, there were two types of women depicted in films: the blonde, who was always seemingly carefree (dumb) or strong-willed (bitchy), and the brunette, who conveniently was always academic (smart) and quirky (unique).

Magazines were no different, you were either team Paris or Nicole. Then there was the 'Who does Chad Michael Murray prefer? Lindsay or Hilary?' or 'Are you team Blair or Serena? Summer or Marisa? Brooke or Peyton?' I could go on. It's no wonder that women have a complex about other women, that women often find it difficult to get along with other women and can have a desire to compete with our fellow sisters.

We have been inherently raised on the idea that if *she* has something, it is something we don't have. We judge each other way too much. We hurt women, and we say things we regret, and all this prevents us from being a strong tribe. It stops us from having life-affirming and rich friendships. It really isn't a surprise that we fail to find our *Sex and the City* friendships when this is the environment we have grown up with.

The number one issue I am asked about is confidence, but the second is making friends, and this is something I battled with for years. There, I've said it. I struggled to find my tribe, and to build healthy, supportive friendships. So how did I cultivate real, valuable friendships? I'll tell you.

MY TRIBE

In middle school I had a very tight-knit group of friends, and we were inseparable but then I moved back to the UK which was very rough. I was academic and shy, and prefer digging deep with people and one-on-one relationships.

I have always had an inner core telling me what is right and wrong and what would be best for me, so I have always known myself, but that doesn't mean I have always been confident. At this new school I started wearing my own version of an "armour". I have always been a "you can sit with me any time kind of girl", but there I was thrown into a group of people I couldn't mesh with and chose to start eating lunch alone and using the library and books to fill my loneliness. It wasn't even at university that I found my tribe either, and that's okay too. Rather than partying I was building my business, and I much preferred being in the campus library than drinking. Each to their own, but I never quite fitted in. I was always one foot in and one foot out of every group.

My tribe did come about though, after university. Where would I be without my main girls? My squad full of smart, brilliant and kind-hearted women? When you find a true friend, it makes life so much easier. So many times in life, I don't know what I would have done if I hadn't had my group of girlfriends as my cheerleaders; the women you can call at 4am with a problem, those are the friends that matter.

You have to appreciate that you and your friends are on the same team. Those outside of your family that are rooting for your success play a huge role in your life. The people that you surround yourself with help build and shape you into the person that you are. Through the good times and the bad, the wildest of evenings and most beautiful mornings, your friends will be your support system for the long haul, so make sure they will be there for you.

Memories with your friends will be the times you tell your children about so work to mix with individuals from all walks of life, all with their own stories to tell and personalities to share. A good friend can give you a whole new perspective on life.

I met one of my best friends in Italy when I first arrived there at 10 years old – Jerus. We couldn't speak the same language, but we did have the universal communication of kindness. On the first day of school she handed me a letter welcoming me to the country and quickly after we became best friends. She and her younger brother were adopted from Ethiopia and she explained so much about her Ethiopian heritage, and has even taught me to speak some Amharic. She is the most amazing light in my life; as well as trusting and being able to rely on her completely, she has opened up my world incredibly. We are still fantastic friends to this day, through weddings (hers) and babies (still hers) we have been a unit.

> *"Women understand. We may share experiences, make jokes, paint pictures, and describe humiliations that mean nothing to men, but women understand."*
>
> **— Gloria Steinem**

Even though there are billions of people on the planet, we can sometimes be drowning in them and still feel overwhelmed with loneliness. Every day at Smart Girl Tribe headquarters, the writers, team and I naturally make sure everyone is seen and heard, but mainly represented. I make sure that all kinds of women show up on our social media feeds, have their voices heard in our office and are seen as equals because we have a responsibility to make sure that everyone is included. At the end of the day, friendships should be celebrated, and they fill our lives with fun and adventures. Make sure your good friends know the real you, and are people you can enjoy wearing long johns around (my friends in Canada know what I mean) – that you can be comfortable and uncomfortable with them. As much as they see you in your messy attire, you need to let them know your messy self as well.

EXERCISE: FIND YOUR SQUAD

Smart Girl Tribe was built out of a need for community because each one of us requires a strong hype squad. We all should have someone who can see the truth in us when we can't see it in ourselves, someone who tells us we are amazing when we're not feeling like it, and someone to call us out when we are making a mistake.

The easiest way to find more applicants for your tribe is by saying "yes" more often. Plan something to do that will get you out of the house and meeting more people once a week. It can be a get-together with new girlfriends, attending a networking event with others in your industry or just attending a course for the fun of it.

When studying for my master's degree in journalism, we were assigned the task of attending a class or event completely outside of our comfort zone. Being "the girl in the library", I knew the class I would need to sign up for would be something along the lines of burlesque. I was nervous to go but knew my journalistic curiosity (and grade) needed me to do this.

On the day, the other women turned up in sexy leotards with their hair backcombed; they were wearing red lipstick, heels and were ready to go. I didn't know how to dress for such a class and turned up wearing an old baggy t-shirt and thick black tights, it was so much fun though and I met some astounding women. The class itself made me feel empowered and strong, and I was definitely out of my comfort zone. It was no mean feat but completely worth it. By saying yes to that one experience I showed my vulnerable side and had the opportunity to grasp how confident I can be even when put on the spot. I also connected with a new group of strong and confident women who were completely different from the females

I aligned with in other parts of my life. It was liberating to view myself differently. It changed my relationship with myself, and tweaked my ideas of what "my tribe" should be.

The other way to extend your reach is online. In my last two years of secondary school, I didn't have a tribe around me, I didn't have the lifetime friendships I was craving, and I didn't have them at university. When I wasn't studying or hanging out in the *BathImpact* office, I was building my business, and nobody got me. "Come out, Scarlett, it's a Saturday night," they would say. But I had a business and was devoted to it; that was the one thing I wanted to spend my time with more than anything. The truth is, going out every night wasn't really me, and I was dreaming of having an office, an international team, and for Smart Girl Tribe to be award-winning. I knew that wasn't going to happen from a nightclub. Of course I did socialise with friends but not as regularly as others. Three times a week hanging in a nightclub just wasn't my idea of fun.

When we later created a Smart Girl Tribe account on Instagram I found myself connecting with other female entrepreneurs, women who were struggling to find their tribe as much as I was. It was through social media that I found people who spoke my language: personal development, women's rights and travel. Use social media to find and hang out in the groups that aren't so readily accessible to you.

Most women just want to be seen and that's possible thanks to social media. No matter what you geek out about (we all have something), you can find it with a few taps on a keyboard – if you haven't found your tribe yet, that doesn't mean you won't. If you can't find tangible real-life women, one of the reasons I love social media is because you can connect with people from all over the world, you can find blogs and conferences and people who love the same thing that you do. Finding others like you is really easy to do online, like my fellow fempreneurs on social media. Don't give up – your *Sex and the City* friendships are out there.

Let's be honest, it would be easier if you could just pick a good friend up at the shop, if you could walk in and say: "I need a best friend, one who is trustworthy, loyal and fierce." But that of course is not possible, so instead I am going to share what I look for in a friend: I choose friends who share similar values and common goals. I call them my purpose partners – we encourage and push each other to fully embrace our individual motives in life.

For traits that you can always find in a good friend, remember the acronym:

Friendly
Respectful
Integrity
Encouraging
Natural
Diligent

It might sound trivial, but think about if you had to write a job description for your friend – would those around you fit the bill? We talk so much about what we look for in a partner, but nobody discusses friendships in the same way. Why not write your own acronym and think about what is important in your own friendships.

FRIENDSHIPS THAT STOP WORKING

An unsupportive friend is a toxic friend, and just as you would in a relationship, you need to break up with that girl or woman. According to a recent survey, 80 per cent of women have had a toxic female friend, so don't worry about being alone in this.

Toxic relationships and friendships are hugely detrimental to our lives and confidence so you need to register the signs early on to be able to nip them in the bud. Life is too short and too beautiful to have unsupportive or manipulative friends who will either discourage you from going after your dream or hold on to your success and live vicariously through you.

They might be someone to judge you, gossip behind your back or even make it their mission to be in competition with you. You might not even realize that a relationship has turned toxic or unhealthy, so every so often take a view, pause for a minute and ask yourself what you are hoping for from your friendships.

Once we have found our friends, sometimes we evolve in a way that changes the relationship. I am all for evolving and becoming the best versions of ourselves, but some friends struggle with that. I had a fantastic friend throughout my university years – notice I said *had*. We were practically attached at the hip, our values were the same and we both were building online platforms. Jasmin had started hers years before Smart Girl Tribe though so when I started getting invited to exclusive blogging events and parties, she was a little jealous. No matter how many times I invited her along, Jasmin wasn't interested. One evening, she pulled me aside after a lecture and told me we could no longer be friends. Why? Because apparently seeing me do so much was making her feel as though she wasn't doing enough. It hit me like a train. The "break-up" affected me for an entire year. It's one thing having a boyfriend say you're too ambitious for his liking, but a best friend? My ride or die? I did learn from that experience though. Never dim your light for someone else, putting out your fire won't keep others warm. Don't stop being yourself for a "friendship".

The media has perpetuated an image that we should be pitting ourselves against each other, and some women will do that naturally. They will decide to put themselves in competition with you and that's unfortunate for everyone. We witness healthy competitiveness every day in the sporting arena but it is a dangerous form of competition when girls compete with you out of jealousy and spite. I have had my fair share of women trying to compete with me but I focus on me, my lane. If a woman is competing with you to the point they are making it their mission to bring you down, look at the source. Where is that behaviour and attitude stemming from? Is there an inner and fundamental reason why they feel less than?

We need to embrace women more, and approach successful women differently. And I promise you this, sister – every bully and toxic woman I have encountered has since called me for a coffee or a position at Smart Girl Tribe. So I promise you, no matter how far away those mean girls seem and how much they bullied you, made fun of you

Decide whether those around you are *stops* or *stays*.

or commented on you, they are watching your success and happiness.

See their nastiness as a compliment and use it to motivate you to up your game further. Looking back, if I am honest, I am grateful to every single bully or mean girl. They motivated me and pushed me to go after the dreams I had, and to strengthen my core value to have grace in my response to them.

Finally, know that if you want a good friendship then you must be a good friend yourself. Building an active soldiery of women who you can take with you is life-altering.

SMART GIRL ACTIONS

- Figure out what type of mean girl you are associating yourself with – try the Who is Your Nemesis? exercise to understand where your bully is coming from.
- Read through the Find Your Squad exercise and plan how you are going to put this into action over the next four weeks.
- Choose personality over popularity. Sometimes we want to fit in so badly that we compromise our integrity. Years after school, university or the job you are in, those bullies won't matter, but you will still be living with yourself, your decisions and your regrets. If you feel yourself succumbing to peer pressure, stop yourself before it's too late. Choose integrity over being popular and you'll find your tribe who will value you and what you stand for, even if those people aren't in your secondary school or at your current job...
- Download some friendship-friendly or hobby-related apps to find people outside your immediate circle or even town.

CHAPTER 5

I PROMISE TO BE CONFIDENT AND LOVE MYSELF UNCONDITIONALLY

Italian women are unlike other European women. As much as you may think that going to the beach with your best girlfriends for a laugh and some fun is easy, preparing for a trip to the beach in Italy is a national sporting event. It takes months of working out, waxing and stripping every hair from your body beforehand. They're practically seals; hairless and smooth. Don't get me started on the time it takes to choose a bikini either. Italians hibernate all throughout the winter. I used to think it was because of the cold, but they are actually getting ready for a season that typically lasts five months (May-September) but seems like a lifetime.

We moved to Italy when I was 10, just shy of those critical pubertal years, also known as the hell years. When you're 13, you start going to the beach as an "Italian" teen, and I was completely unaware of the prerequisites for an Italian beach. (I am White British and this means pale – as close to transparent as you can be.) Arriving at the train station, my two girlfriends Lucia and Giulia were waxed, stripped and glowing. I was wearing my British attire: a loose-fitting cotton white kaftan and a large hat with a circumference grand enough to cover up all my sins and my bikini, which had been put away for a year or so. (Have you ever noticed that British beaches look like 80s infomercials as that's how long everyone's beach gear has been hiding in the closet because it is never sunny in England?) Being the only blonde on the beach, not only was I not confident but I couldn't hide behind a bookshelf now.

Italians parade on the beach, walking up and down the coast calling it "exercise"; it's more a clever tactic to lure in guys. You walk up and down, showing off your seal-like body, smiling and hoping to attract a suitor. I would sit in the shade, plastering on the factor 50 and rotating to the opposite direction of the sun. While my best girlfriends danced in the sea and practised cartwheels I hid under my tent-like kaftan and watched as everyone else had fun.

***

No matter what event I am speaking at, given that I am jumping around, jumping up and down to girl power anthems talking about important issues and preaching that your dream can come true with enough perseverance and tenacity, audiences tend to assume that I'm super-confident. The truth is though that the "girl in the library" was never that way. I have always known myself well enough to know what I stand for, but being confident is a whole other kettle of fish.

Confidence isn't pre-made. You're not born with confidence, it is a skill that most of us have to harness to show up as our best selves. No woman will ever wake up every morning thinking, "This is it. I am confident." Though if you are one of those women, then go you. You're fabulous and should definitely be spreading more confidence dust around.

One scroll on Instagram, one throwback photo or even a look in the mirror on the wrong day can still send me into a spiral of self-doubt and negative thoughts. Maybe my hair looks particularly shiny in a post or my travels look splendidly glamorous, but I am not perfect and neither am I striving to be. It's important you know this right now.

BE BODY POSITIVE
Our bodies are certainly one of the first things tied up with our confidence, and for me, I would be devastated if you couldn't value your body and its power. Yes, I booked my first waxing appointment after that dreaded day at the beach (or hilarious day, depending on how you look at it), but what sticks with

me is how much I missed out on that day because I wasn't confident in myself, not throwing caution to the wind. I was surrounded by my friends, but more concerned with how my hair stood out than them, more focused on hiding my body than the laughs we could have been having, and my terrible outfit rather than being in the sea. If I could go back and say one thing to that girl it would be: "you need to love yourself and your shape". So much has changed for me since that day. Now I'm the first one in the sea and the last to go home and I enjoy every second, without even thinking about my appearance.

My whole life is based on empowering other women to thrive, to be their best selves. It can be difficult considering the amount of negative information we are still being fed, yet I persist. Last month, I was looking after my friend's 11-year-old daughter. She likes it when I teach her how to say different things in one of the six languages I know. I asked her to draw herself to teach her all the body parts in the different languages I speak. Her response broke my heart. She said, "Scarlett, I am going to draw myself skinnier because I'll be happier."

Excuse me. This incredibly talented and kind-hearted girl was telling me she wasn't good enough how she was. Having a myriad of problems with this statement, I explained to her that skinniness never equals happiness, and beauty is found within. You've heard that before, right?

Listen up, you might think about how much more confident you would be without acne or adult braces, or without short legs or curly hair, but even if you didn't have those things, there would still be other things you wouldn't like about yourself, which is why we are nipping this in the bud. Don't we have better things to be talking about and graver issues to face? As Coco Chanel said: "Beauty starts the moment you decide to be yourself."

Isn't this the whole bloody point of why I started Smart Girl Tribe? Rather than your body, let's talk about changing our lives or the world. Instead of talking about our hip or pant size or our not-so-visible thigh gap (or not visible at all), let's talk about women's rights or how divisive the world is becoming.

Deprivation, planning, comparing: these are a waste of valuable time. It's not our fault – the most attractive children and people are in our faces on television shows and in advertising. With white teeth, shiny hair and zero per cent body fat, they have been photoshopped, preened and prepped and that's where the damaging message starts. Let me tell you – you won't be remembered for your lack of cellulite or the size of your pores. Your worth isn't increased as your dress size decreases, you can't have a conversation with abs and no hairstyle can change the world.

The thing I love most about my body is what it can do. Our legs can power us around tracks and our arms around swimming pools. Our bodies take us to places where there are amazing experiences to be had and memories to be made. Not forgetting to mention that our whole beings are designed to grow and keep a baby alive – wow, a silent applause for all the mothers out there. As a side note, you are not less than or any less special if you're not able to bear a child.

Thank your body for all of that. Especially as women, our bodies can do remarkable things, which are far too often overlooked because we are busy comparing bra, butt, nose or even finger sizes.

We weigh more than a number calculated on a device, more than our thighs or tummy or arms: our weight is how heavy we are in the world – the mark we are making, the way we speak to and treat people. If you work out – and I beg you to because it gets all the happy vibes going – then aim to be strong so you can defend yourself from the negative views of others, set out to be fierce so you can slay your dreams and be graceful so that you can always hold your own.

Self-confidence is the best outfit, ice-breaker, friend-attracter and way to improve your day, so own it. Your worth cannot be measured, it is infinite. Hating and loathing yourself is only going to take up space in your head, room that you should be using to grow your life. We need to practise self-acceptance and not take part in the problem that has

You are stuck with the only person you can't get rid of, so be kind to yourself.

destroyed so many lives. This conversation has to keep going for change to actually occur, and we each have our part to play in that.

EXERCISE: CELEBRATE YOURSELF

I want you to find one photo of yourself. On the back, write everything you are good at and features you love about yourself, not just your physical qualities though – your emotional and mental strengths and skills too. I expect you to run out of space because you are listing so many things.

Keep it on your bedside table and then, any morning you feel in need of extra confidence, look at this photo and read the words on the back. It's an instant mood changer, and will help you feel as though you can rule the world.

COMPARISON

Comparing yourself to others can totally steal your confidence. I could spend so much time thinking about how I'm not shaped like a supermodel, but I know that supermodels are comparing themselves to someone else too – it's a vicious circle. Let's be honest, I would rather be reading and developing my business than thinking about whether or not I have a thigh gap. Wouldn't you?

It has also become ten times harder as a consequence of social networks. Social media is the Wild West with no policing, and now we have a multitude of zero per cent body fat, detoxing girls letting us know how we can buy into that concept and have the perfect everything like them. Girls, I'm basically Italian and, as every girl knows, size zero just isn't worth wasting any pasta for.

As soon as you start comparing yourself to someone else, you are doing your own identity a disservice. As a woman, maybe a part of us will look at the woman next to us but I promise you that *that* woman is comparing herself to the woman next to her as well. Being *you* is your superpower, really. You and your thoughts can't be duplicated and the way you are – that special something about you – that can never be replicated. That is magic.

DIMINISHING OURSELVES

Another huge confidence problem we face as women is our tendency to shrink ourselves and hide our accomplishments. I have gone through periods of being so uncomfortable speaking about my job, dumbing it down and calling it small – but the only thing I was doing was talking myself down and doing myself (and the world) an injustice.

A few years into Smart Girl Tribe, thousands of women were reading the magazine and I was being flown around the world to speak, yet talking about it always felt boastful to me. My character didn't seem to match my dreams – those reveries were huge but I kept putting myself down. It was only at a party when a friend introducing me to someone couldn't really describe my job, because I never really opened up about it, that I noticed the damaging impact making myself seem small was having.

That was when I had an epiphany, recognizing that I wasn't helping anyone by diminishing myself and my talent. Imagine if I had carried on with that mentality of shrinking myself. Picture how many lives I wouldn't have changed, how many events wouldn't have happened, how many people I wouldn't have transformed. Don't live as half of yourself – you are your best advocate.

Many of us have grown up being encouraged to be small and give room to others. It's no surprise that we are natural people-pleasers. We are actively pushed to not be "too" anything in case we could be deemed threatening, overpowering or intimidating. Honey, you're not intimidating – *they* are just intimidated. This isn't an easy conversation to have, it makes people uncomfortable – both men and women – but that doesn't mean we should be dismissing problems

Be so confident and full of love for yourself that you don't have time to think of anything but what kind of person you want to be, and your legacy.

around gender, or not questioning the status quo. I refuse to teach the leaders of tomorrow this narrative.

Start thinking of people as snowflakes – each of us is crafted in an entirely once-in-a-lifetime way. As a result of social media and magazines, where everyone is digitally enhanced, there is an enormous amount of pressure to look a certain way. Aren't you tired of this? I am exhausted. Every time you want to change yourself to be like someone else, or you dumb yourself down, you disappoint the woman within you who could be doing so much more.

According to powerhouse Melissa Ambrosini, the bestselling author and host of *The Melissa Ambrosini Show*, every decision we make comes from a place of either love or fear – from the way we look at ourselves in the mirror to the clothes we choose. Are you wearing particular outfits because you feel great inside? Or because you think that's what you should be wearing and you fear standing out from the crowd? Do you style your hair according to your lifestyle or your personal choice? Are you moving your body to celebrate or punish it? Are you nourishing your body with foods that light you up or that you know aren't good for you?

The words *should, if* and *when* are words I detest: "if I lose the weight, I'll be happy". "When I am rich, life will be better." If you are living by *if, when* or *should*, you will never be happy. If you are living according to what you should be wearing, how you should be acting, or what you should be doing, you will never be living on your terms. Everything you do achieve will be for nothing because you're not being honest, or true to yourself. If you do complete or accomplish those things, you will replace them with something else that you think is stopping you from reaching your full potential. You will always be a step away from where and who you think you need to be if you judge yourself against others.

Here are some tools that I want to share with you, practices I have implemented in my life to become more confident and accepting of who I am – to help me deal with intimidating situations and to control those internal doubts for good.

PREPARE FOR BATTLE

Being prepared is an easy confidence booster because it helps you take on a situation with poise. Before a scary meeting, talk or interview, stand like Wonder Woman outside for a few seconds – shoulders back, hands on hips. Standing tall and strong like a warrior is a power pose and will help you feel and radiate confidence. The purpose is to take up space and not lessen yourself.

The Wonder Woman pose is a high power pose you can also do in the morning when you get up. It will boost your day and is super-easy.

"You have been criticizing yourself for years, and it hasn't worked. Try approving of yourself and see what happens."

— Louise L. Hay

YOUR INNER MEAN GIRL

Have you ever complimented someone and they haven't agreed? Have you ever told a friend she is a brilliant leader or has a beautiful smile but she can't see it? To be confident, above anything else you need to demolish your inner mean girl, the one mean girl we can't escape.

Every female has an inner mean girl, a voice inside us that sabotages, rather than supports. She is the force that lives in your head and feeds you negative thoughts and energy. If your best friend was telling you about her failures, how much she despises her thighs or how she is not good enough, you wouldn't stand for that, would you? Then why the heck are you talking to yourself like that, and letting yourself get away with it?

Be your encouraging and compassionate best friend in your head and stop telling yourself all these lies on repeat. Our inner critic may seem like a part of us, but the truth is that she isn't the real you. She uses distortions and untruths to talk down to you, to convince you you're not enough, that you should be doing more or that you'll never be able to achieve your goals.

Your inner mean girl is just a reflection of the things that you fear most, your biggest worries and vulnerabilities. For example, when I was preparing for my university year abroad in Rome, I was petrified and tried everything to get out of going. My inner mean girl kept telling me that I would be lonely, that I wouldn't make any friends. She was reflecting exactly what I was most anxious about, and that kind of thinking nearly sabotaged my success. After a lot of internal discussions, disputes and mentally murdering my inner mean girl, I set off for Rome and savoured every minute. From living with my best friend to exploring the capital by night and living out my Audrey Hepburn dream, I never could have dreamed how magnificent those months were.

If you want to stop the cycle of self-abuse and self-loathing, then separate yourself from that mean girl and introduce a cycle of compassion and self-love. Start talking to your inner mean girl – tell her to back off. Aim to shut her down before she gets going, and remember that nobody else can hear what your inner mean girl says so don't give her any attention by repeating what she thinks out loud. Focus on being your enchanting self without listening to her for one second.

One tool I practise is naming my inner mean girl. Becoming aware of your negative inner voice is the first step to silencing it, so by separating that voice from your own and naming it, you understand it is not the real you talking. Being named Scarlett, I chose to call my inner mean girl Sheila (no disrespect to any Sheilas out there). As soon as my inner mean girl starts saying something to me, I turn around and shut the door on her, as though she is a real person. I refuse to give her power or space in my head and life.

For years, I was asked to speak at public events. People would email or call me to say how motivational and inspiring my content was, and that my story deserved to be told.

Large gulp

As flattering as it was , "Sheila" kept getting in the way. She persisted in telling me to just stay in my lane and that I wasn't loud or worthy enough to be a speaker.

After reading a book, one which asks you to tackle your fears head on, I knew that it was time to learn to manage this irrational fear of mine. What was the worst that could happen? Did I think people would laugh, or regret hiring me? Did I really believe it would mean my career failing and everyone knowing me as *that* girl? Images of Lizzie McGuire tripping at her middle school graduation came to mind. No, I had to do this, or at least try. I was flooded with images and concerns from Sheila, who was telling me everything that could go wrong, but I decided to take that chance.

The following day, I phoned the school closest to my house and asked for the opportunity to speak about my business journey and the greatest lessons I had learned. On the day, the head informed me that they had initially sent around an email to 40 students but once word had spread, 400 students wanted to turn up to listen to me.

As I sat at the front, about to take to the podium, I scanned the room of faces staring back at me, going over my final notes in my head. There was no turning back. Nobody warned me of the nearest exit as they do on planes, there was no life jacket to support me if things went wrong. This was it.

"You have to choose the thing you are most scared of, just to prove that you can do it," is how I started my presentation as I mentally squashed Sheila triumphantly.

Imagine how many students would have missed out on my speeches if I *had* listened to Sheila though? You could be changing the world too, if only you stopped listening to your inner mean girl.

Close the door on her. When we listen to our inner mean girl, we are letting her drive instead of putting her in her place. If you let your Sheila drive, she is going to crash into a ditch or a wall. You need to drop her off at a petrol station somewhere, where she can stay forever.

No matter how many fantastic relationships you have in your life, the most important one is the relationship you have with yourself, so live and make decisions from a perspective of love, not fear.

EXERCISE: MIRROR AFFIRMATIONS

A long time ago I noticed how kind I can be to others but so rarely to myself, so I set myself a task. For 30 days after I woke up, I would say something nice to the first reflection of myself I saw. Sometimes it would be my phone, other times it would be the mirror in my bedroom or bathroom as I was brushing my teeth.

Initially, it felt awkward to say one nice thing about myself every day but then I noticed the positive effect it was having on my self-esteem. Some days I would be appreciative of my ambitions. Another day I would simply thank my eyebrows for looking more like sisters than enemies.

I urge you to take up this challenge yourself for 30 days. Commit to saying one nice thing about yourself as soon as you see your reflection in the morning and over time it will become a habit. Habits shape your life, sister, so implement healthy ones.

VULNERABILITY

Another trick to combat your inner mean girl is in finding and showing your vulnerability. This might feel counterintuitive, but being vulnerable means being soft, and you need to show others, especially those who might be looking up to you, that gentle (and real) doesn't mean weak.

True strength comes from vulnerability, compassion and honesty. Many women think strength is thinking: "I don't need anyone, I am fine." But that's not necessarily strong. Loving and connecting is strength, and acknowledging how remarkable another woman is. We don't do that enough.

Often we try to hide our "weakness", our vulnerable side, but it is through vulnerability that true connection, friendship and love arise. Vulnerability for you might mean stepping up and finally launching your business, or allowing yourself to fall deeply and truly in love. It might be having a hard conversation or talking about feelings. As Brené Brown says: "Every story of courage is completely underpinned by vulnerability, you can't get to courage without walking through vulnerability."

We all have stories and truths that, if exposed to others, we worry would result in people mocking or judging us. Vulnerability and the revelation of our weaknesses allow us to connect more to our most authentic selves, though, and doing so humanizes us. You might think that sharing your story is going to metaphorically strip you naked, which makes you vulnerable, but those stories are what render it safe for others to unburden themselves. We need to look at other women and say, "Hey, I am in this too."

***

To embrace confidence, start with yourself and choose to set the example of compassion and understanding. Launching Smart Girl Tribe meant doing something entirely different to all of my friends and essentially everyone I knew. Nobody really understood it, but I chose to set an example for others to look up to. I knew this would be the most vulnerable choice and the most scary and difficult path, but it also hugely boosted my confidence.

Be the reason why another woman starts to feel confident in herself. Accept yourself, including all of your flaws. Let the beauty you have within you shine through to radiate sincerity and the most authentic you.

SMART GIRL ACTIONS

- Select your "Celebrate Yourself" photograph and place it where you will see it every day as a reminder of your strengths and attributes – the things that make you stand out.
- Complete your Mirror Affirmations for 30 days to notice an uplift in the way you view yourself.
- Use the Wonder Woman pose before any stressful or worrying situation.
- Do one big thing that scares you this year. Pushing yourself out of your comfort zone is good for your self-esteem, and will give you a warm buzz afterwards as you congratulate yourself for being strong and uniquely you.

CHAPTER 6

I PROMISE TO BE A TOTAL #BOSS

Farrah Storr was the poster girl of cool, and the editor of *Cosmopolitan*. There she was on the blue banner, her grin twinkling away at me.

I was in the middle of London staring in on a room where cliques of women were sipping on champagne and nibbling on canapes, the type that are only offered at special events. Even from the outside, through the formidable glass windows, I could see each seat with the latest edition of *Cosmopolitan* propped on it.

The steward was signing each attendee in, taking their name and scanning their confirmation email. Clearly, these women (and the few men) had been invited exclusively to see Farrah Storr, a TED speaker and author. What were the odds of me getting in with no ticket? No reservation? No confirmation email? Slim to none. Would that stop me? Heck, no. I wasn't going to let this preppy steward intimidate me. I had semi-made it in the Big Apple after all.

Knowing I had to execute this with confidence, and metaphorically putting on my big girl pants, I stood tall and pulled out my phone and pretended to be on the phone to someone major. Victoria Beckham? DVF? Who knows.

"Of course, not a problem at all. I will make sure the plane is booked for ten." I hurried to the front of the queue, with attitude and sass, smiling sweetly at the women queuing. There was no spite in what I was trying to achieve, I was just a 22-year-old who intended to make the most of this opportunity. Smart Girl Tribe began as a journalistic endeavour and I knew exactly who Farrah Storr was.

At the front, I whispered to the steward that I was working in the building and had left my bag in there. At 22 I only carried a phone and lip-gloss with me so knew this story could be remotely convincing. Sighing, he signalled me in.

Indoors was white, immaculate, with screens everywhere and a room set up in theatre style. There stood Farrah chatting away to the organizer about her presentation. Quickly sitting, I put my hair in a pony and took off my blazer, praying that the steward wouldn't recognize me if he were to make an appearance at any point.

Being a boss means knowing your worth, being willing to take a risk to reach your dreams, having clarity and learning to stand up for yourself when someone says "no".

Post-talk, I literally ran up to Farrah and in the space of 16 seconds spewed my résumé and articulated my grit and tenacity in moving to New York. Leaving Farrah with my number and email address, the next morning she confirmed I could come into the *Cosmopolitan* offices.

My time at *Cosmo* was a lot of fun and everything you could imagine it to be. This is just one of the many times I have thrown myself into deep water and prayed it would work out (it wasn't the only time I sneaked into an event).

This chapter is to share the lessons I learned and the advice I wish was imparted to me at 19 when launching, at 21 when I went full-time and later when, according to societal standards, I had "made it". I was never a child to sell sweets in the playground and, if I am being completely honest, I still don't know what a business proposal is. Smart Girl Tribe has been modelled under my leadership for sure, but I have had to learn on the job.

Let me say it again for those in the back, you do not need to have your own business or company to be entrepreneurial. Whether you are hoping to become an author, surgeon, professional speaker or founder of a media empire, here is an insight into the greatest lessons I have learned along the way to becoming a success in business.

TEN PRINCIPLES TO BUSINESS SUCCESS

1. ENGAGEMENT

There are two types of people in the world: those who walk into a room saying "here I am", and those who walk into a room saying "here *you* are". I want you to be one of those who focus on who is already in the room, who you are speaking to. For anyone to want to buy in to your product or service, you need to be interested in them; that will only happen if you engage with them.

At the heart of engagement is defining your client – you need to know where they're hanging out, what influencers they follow and their go-to coffee order. You could have millions of followers and likes, but your audience needs to engage and align with your brand and company in order to create a meaningful relationship that builds community and revenue.

I started this book and will end it stressing how *you* are the whole reason to my being. You are the answer to all my questions: what does the reader want? What is the reader struggling with? How can I help the reader more? No matter how egotistical your business seems, it will always be about providing a service and resolving a problem. A great tip for this is to research your followers, take note of the issues they are talking about and the language they are using and mirror it in your own business and account. Your clients and customers will want to relate to you, so by using the same language as them and highlighting their issues in your Instagram Story or on your grid will instantly solidify this intention.

2. CREATE VALUE

Your business is only as valuable as the worth that you bring to other people and their lives. I have only been able to travel the world and be invited to Harvard because of word-of-mouth. For years, I wasn't just generating content, uploading pretty Instagram images and retweeting quotes, but heavily talking to my readers, directing them to resources that could help their mental health, putting them in touch with fellow business owners to help them secure an internship, and even driving to their towns for mini-meet-ups. It's because of those little yet powerfully valuable actions that now those meet-ups have turned into an entire event series and those mental health tips have led us to being finalists in the UK Mental Health blog awards. When you start a business, it should be to resolve a problem or to help someone; don't set up a business for the money. Remember what I said earlier: "Anything worth having takes a long time, and anything taking a long time is worth having." *That*.

Whether it's being true to your brand or your personal style, authenticity is the secret to any kind of success.

3. AUTHENTICITY

A few months into building Smart Girl Tribe I noticed how impactful other more career-focused websites were and I had a "ground-breaking" idea that Smart Girl Tribe should become exactly that. We started exclusively focusing on business content and, girl, was that a mistake. Our numbers plummeted, readers were confused and I struggled to feel as passionate about the site as usual. So we did a quick U-turn and went back to being our most authentic selves, to talking about mental health, feminism and personal development alongside careers. I'm deeply happy that I realized straight away that changing the core of Smart Girl Tribe was a mistake.

SGT's tagline is: "to encourage women to become their most fearless and authentic selves", because that's where the beauty lies.

In being authentic, remember not to underestimate your feminine traits. I've had years of being told to be more aggressive (like a man), stubborn (like a man), and a bulldozer (like a man). That never sat right with me and as soon as I started leaning in to my natural tendencies, to being compassionate and empathic, sensitive and nurturing, which felt more natural to me, the happier in business I became. Which is ultimately the meaning to life – to be happy.

4. THINK OF WHAT SETS YOU APART

Standing out goes way beyond being authentic. One day, I was invited to a female entrepreneur meet-up in London and a bright young woman pulled me aside wanting to discuss Smart Girl Tribe. She, too, wanted to create a female empowerment organization and I happily (and naively) obliged and opened up about our journey, our vision and what makes the business so great. A few days later she sent me a link to her website – it was the same as mine, and the copy and the images were too similar for my liking. I wasn't upset, just disappointed that here was a young woman brimming with talent yet she felt the need to copy our entire company. We bumped into each other at another event a few weeks later and she admitted to her wrongdoing, saying that she had shut down her website quickly because it wasn't taking her anywhere. She wasn't truly interested because she wasn't thinking about the unique talents and ideas *she* had.

My USP is that I was, and still am, completely normal. I could have been anyone, just a normal person you walk past in your local coffee shop and that's not something I wanted to lose. Figure out what the one thing setting you apart is and go all in on it. Perhaps it's your visual approach or your business' tone of voice. Perhaps it's the medium in which you communicate

with your audience. Identify how you can stand out in an
authentic and engaging manner. Think about the gaps in the
market, the service or product you could offer and how it
would shake up the industry.

5. GET EDUCATED

You have the business and the audience, you're providing
value and engaging your audience all while being authentic.
Now it's time to learn – to upgrade your knowledge and
develop the right mindset to generate *more* success.

Years into Smart Girl Tribe, I was about to launch an
exclusive area for members. I knew Smart Girl Tribe could build
it but I didn't know where to start, so I started reading Carrie
Green's *She Means Business*, a book which has become a staple
in the Smart Girl Tribe goodie bags. Other business books I
consider my staples include *Unleash the Giant Within* by Tony
Robbins, *Work Party* by Jaclyn Johnson, and Stephen Covey's
The 7 Habits of Highly Effective People. I'm also no stranger to
podcasts, which are an easy way to tune out of the world
and regain motivation, I adore Cressida Bonas's podcast on
fear and Elizabeth Day on failure. The Editor-in-Chief of *Stylist*
magazine Lisa Smosarski also recently recommended the
Squiggly Career podcast which will help you establish your
values (more on that later in the self-care chapter).

Educating yourself is fundamental. Reading is great for developing yourself and your business, and you also need to develop tangible entrepreneurial talents such as networking, negotiation and leadership.

I love to constantly learn, which is why I persevered when learning languages. Living in Italy meant learning Spanish, French, Latin and Russian in Italian. It has taken pure determination to learn the tenses, understand the vocabulary and build the confidence to actually speak those languages but, living all over the world, my language skills have enabled me to embrace foreign cultures and diverse people, explore exotic foods and partake in all sorts of activities.

Trust me, if I can dedicate a lifetime to embrace six languages, you have the power in you to educate yourself every day too. Whether you are a business owner or employed, invest time every day in continuing your education.

6. MAX OUT ON YOUR DREAMS

Now that you are surrounded by resources, the worst thing you could do is to choose one small goal. That goal is going to be accomplished, and fast. And then what?

When I started, my goal was to create a digital magazine. I achieved that on day one of launching Smart Girl Tribe. If I had only stayed with that one goal, I wouldn't be where I am today.

Have the audacity to dream big. Slowly but surely over the years I have dreamed up and achieved some gigantic goals on my list – speaking at Harvard, launching an event series and writing a book. They each came true because I committed to maxing out on my dreams, not shrinking my thoughts and letting those self-limiting thoughts take over.

You might not be there yet, but that doesn't mean you won't ever be. Decide what your greatest, most vibrant life would look like and work backwards. On smartgirltribe.com there is a fantastic meditation for this kind of work, called "meditation to manifesting your dream life". It is the guided visualization I turn to when I need some extra sparkly dust to keep me believing I can do and have it all (and is free to download).

7. DON'T STICK TO WHAT YOU KNOW

As I have just said, you can dream bigger than you ever thought possible. Did I think I would be travelling the world as an early twenty-something living out my dream life? Heck, no.

It happened because I had the audacity to dream it up. At school, I was brilliant at languages but not so much at maths. I was great at starting a magazine but didn't think I would ever be able to organize events for Smart Girl Tribe or become a speaker, yet here we are. It's similar with your career. Put one foot in front of the other and complete your 5-5-5 Exercise, asking: "What could I be doing today to get me closer to where I want to be tomorrow?" When you're conjuring up your dreams and goals, don't just stick to what you know in that very present moment, you'll be doing yourself a disservice.

Smart Girl Tribe started as a magazine, but we now have a members' area and top-rated podcast. I never once had doubts about staying in my lane. I'm inspired by individuals such as Reese Witherspoon: she is an actress, activist, fashion designer and has a book and media company. She clearly never thought she had to box herself in.

8. BEING READY IS A LIE

What are you putting off because you don't want to be a beginner? Choose a "Day One" and be willing to start somewhere. That is why many women fail to make their dreams a reality. You don't have to be an expert, have the right equipment or years of experience. Nothing bad will happen if only three women show up to your event, nothing will happen if only a dozen people listen to your podcast for its first season. Ask yourself where in your business or in life you need to choose a Day One? Do you need to be willing to stumble? That is where you need to start before

Whenever someone tells you "no", figure out if this means "not yet", "not you", or "not this idea."

you are ready. If there are only a few people watching you, that's great because it means you get to practise. You get to mess up and learn. You get to try again, and fail forward. Absolutely everyone has to start from zero. It's not the smartest woman in the room who wins, but the woman who goes all in.

9. PERSEVERE

There is a special place in my heart where SGT resides. I am often asked what the secret is. How was it that a year after secondary school I was able to build a fully fledged company?

The simple answer is perseverance. I never listened when someone said no, and I didn't take it personally. I churned all the challenges and disappointments and flipped them. With any negative response, I have tried to learn something, asking myself: what is the lesson here? What can I take away from this to help me and the company grow?

Many ideas of mine have been rejected over the years, but as an aspiring entrepreneur you have to get used to hearing no. I often tell audiences that there are thousands of women who could be in my position today, but the difference is that I haven't backed down or given up. I have risen after every failure, stood up again after every setback and got into the ring even when I didn't have any evidence to suggest I would be successful in doing so. You can too.

10. BE OKAY BEING THE 1%

Sadly, 99% of people won't pursue their dream with all of their energy and commitment. They will have excuses as to why it's not right or not working for them. Set goals that will serve you and your business, and don't expect it to happen straight away. Talk to anyone successful – what might look like an overnight success story was realistically years in the making. People just see accolades.

I was 19 when I was started my business, yes – a teenager. A great load of naivety came with this, and as you know, it didn't exactly make me a party girl at university. I spent evenings heading up to London for networking events and even declined invitations to gigs and nights out to transcribe my university notes.

Admittedly, I zoned out in class and would be thinking about Smart Girl Tribe, the business and my vision for it. Notebooks for my lectures were filled with bright ideas and thoughts. I loved it, really loved it. Nothing could pull me away from Smart Girl Tribe and this community I had built. Nobody could convince me that a cocktail with friends would be better than my darkened room and going through my next set of article ideas.

The walls of my dorm were full of quotes and motivational posters, my desk drawers were crammed with books on being an entrepreneur, and my iTunes playlist was a stream of girl power anthems to keep me going way past midnight. If you follow me on Spotify, you will know exactly what songs I am referring to.

Don't let fear or self-doubt get to you. Doubt is a dream killer, as with other people's opinions. Those who love you want to protect you and they'll want you to play it safe. Nobody, though, has ever created an extraordinary life by staying within the lines.

Fear is often an indication of what you should do, not what you shouldn't do. I have been scared for most of my career. If I am not scared I start to worry that I am not challenging myself with new things. You might have a fear of failing – "newsflash": rock bottom is six levels lower than you think, and it's dark there. But it's riskier to not follow your dreams than to fail, I promise you. I have always identified as an independent woman, one in a long line of women who failed before they succeeded. I know that doesn't make it easier, but find solace in knowing that failing is a shared experience with your role models.

Everything you have ever started began with a first time, so don't be afraid of venturing into new territory. When it comes to Olympians, award-winning entrepreneurs, bestselling authors or Academy Award winners, remember they never started off being those things. Be the 1%.

"Nothing will work unless you do."

— **Maya Angelou**

WAYS TO START
Thanks to some insanely talented businesswomen paving the way, we are now the generation standing up and not afraid to say we want it all and can have it all. This is my official invitation to you to consider having your own business or to learn more about running a business as a woman.

No successful entrepreneur these days has followed a preordained path. And if you are just starting out, this is a blessing in disguise. My best piece of advice would be to not set out to be "an entrepreneur", or even "a successful entrepreneur". Decide what the word "entrepreneur" looks like for you. Determine what your passion is, and ask yourself how you can serve with excellence. Often we end up as entrepreneurs because the job we want doesn't actually exist and neither does the position.

Was I born an entrepreneur? No. You can condition yourself to become a wildly successful business owner, though – I am proof of that. You can train yourself to be a talented, thriving and exceptional boss.

There isn't a difference between you and me. You have the tools I had. I made the choice to go to university, and maybe you're not in that position, but if I hadn't gone to university I would have had those four extra years to focus on my business. See the positive in whatever choices you make – change your narrative to be the businesswoman you want to be. If you were looking for a sign to tell yourself otherwise, then you've come to the wrong place because here we lift each other up.

Don't let your lack of experience hold you back either. I was a teenager and had less than no experience when I started. Trust me – I have created and refined the writing, the website and our social media, through working hard and turning up. If you already have a job, that's not an excuse not to start your very own side hustle. You don't need to create the next Spanx or MacBook, you can start small and you will discover the joys of your own business.

Running a business and watching how it impacts lives is the greatest thing I have ever done. It may be changing your world, but you have changed mine. There isn't a roadmap for building a community and scaling it; you need to try things, explore different voices, and be open to evolving. Consistency will always trump experience. You can be the girl with ten years of experience under her belt, but if you are not reliable or trustworthy, you have nothing. Every day comes with its own share of trials but I can't wait to get to work. Nowadays, there isn't such a thing as a nine to five, and when 75% of our lives is being taken up by work, isn't it our duty to make sure we love our work and that what we are putting into the world is worthy of us?

Consider this an official invitation to join other creative and entrepreneurial women. The only thing that can literally stop you is *you*, just as the only thing that can get you started is you. It's risky going after your dream, but it's riskier not to.

SMART GIRL ACTIONS

- Think about what sets you apart. A lot has been done already in the world but not by you, and that is something to hold on to. View your business idea the same way.
- Research other companies. Look into the businesses that are accomplishing what you want to in different areas, and those at the helm. Look at how they are achieving their stand-out.
- Insist on swerving into other lanes. As women we are multi-faceted, so what makes you think that when it comes to your career it should be any different? When launching your business, you don't need to only be one thing.
- Work through the Ten Principles to look at areas in which you need to develop and understand what your business life could look like.

CHAPTER 7

I PROMISE TO EMBRACE SELF-CARE AND TAKE A WELL-NEEDED PAUSE

Two winters ago, I was working a steady 16 hours a day for seven days a week, wanting to do it all, and completing every task without fail. I rose before the sun each morning, and collapsed into bed around midnight. Having decided I didn't need help, the meetings I couldn't fit in face to face were over Skype or Zoom during my "lunch hour". Taking calls while running from meeting to meeting became my cardio and evenings were spent networking at business events.

Don't get me wrong, my job on any given day means I am a social media manager, speaker, writer, podcaster, YouTuber, CEO, activist, editor, videographer, merchandise designer and event host, among so many other roles, and I love that. While also balancing being a girlfriend, friend, sister, daughter and boss, however, this was too much. I had zero downtime. The candle was burning at both ends, which I was determined to maintain in my desire to keep every plate spinning. Burned out, frazzled and fried, my sorry ass had no energy left. I was spent, dead as a battery. My goals and dreams suddenly seemed unmanageable.

"What do people do when they relax? It's not productive, it's not changing the world. Relaxing does nothing for anyone." That was what I kept telling myself each and every day. All the while, I would say, "I'm fine, I'm totally fine. I haven't slept in nine days, but everything is under control."

I have met you tribers at summits and career events and I know how ambitious you are, how focused you are on achieving your goals, and that one dream isn't enough. This is why we are soul-sisters, because I understand. Have you seen a friend on social media praise her boyfriend and use up her 30 hashtags on Instagram to shout from the rooftops about their "couple goals" and then they've suddenly broken up? We have all been there, and I was no different. On the verge of burning out, I couldn't bring myself to share with others that I was having a testing time.

It was time to be honest, and that meant taking a step back and asking myself not what I wanted, but what I needed. Being so addicted to my job, I wanted to carry on but, instead, I booked a ticket to Ireland. It had always been a pipedream of mine to travel around the South of Ireland. A friend came with me and it was so much fun; we laughed, met the Killarney football team one evening over Guinness, climbed clifftops and really embraced the Irish attitude towards life. I'm under no illusion though that a few weeks' travelling gave me the epiphany I was expecting but I understood deep down that my body was craving a lifestyle change.

Returning from that trip renewed and refreshed, I was armed with my newly purchased range of herbal teas, bath salts and recipes for making my own face masks. You know where this is heading ... After six weeks I was back to my old habits, except that this time I knew I was heading towards burnout again. Teas and a few Epsom salt baths weren't going to help me long term; I needed a complete self-care rethink.

The only way forward was to carve out a year, a full 365 days to build a self-care system, a combination of strong strategies so I would never experience such low self-worth or burnout again.

Imagine a house, and then four pillars holding it up. The house is called "my self-care system" and it is supported by four pillars called **Routines**, **Boundaries**, **Values** and **Self-Worth**. Consider this Self-Care 101 for the ambitious, focused and too-driven-for-her-own-good kind of gal.

I still am constantly moving and "on" at work. While writing this book I was already producing our first international event, and while speaking at Oxford University I was booking my flight to Harvard, but my self-care system is so strong that I now feel empowered and light whatever life throws at me. It is thanks to my system that I feel whole and exude unapologetic optimism. I have no doubt my pillars will do the same for you.

EXERCISE: MY POSITIVE ROUTINE

Every morning, usually in the shower, I ask myself three questions to prime my mind for a positive day: What can I be happy about today? What can I be grateful for today? And how can I respond to any stress or negative feelings in a positive way?

These three questions prompt positive emotions for the rest of the day. Some days, rather than wait until I am in the shower to answer these questions, I ask them as soon as I'm awake. I use doors as reminders too – when I step out of the front door I ask myself the same three questions, when opening my car door I remind myself of the three answers. It helps me relax and approach every day positively.

"Self-care means giving yourself permission to pause."

—Cecelia Tran

Routines are powerful because they are a simple way to introduce a set of gentle actions to consistently improve your overall wellbeing. You can't decide one day that you'll start taking care of yourself and expect you won't fall off the wagon. You will, but that's why you need to have the routine in place to help you get back up.

Before my morning shower, I spend an hour by myself. For 20 minutes I stretch a little or practise yoga, followed by 20 minutes of journalling and then 20 minutes carrying out my 5-5-5 Rule. Refer to Chapter One if you need a refresher on the latter.

As much as we talk about developing a morning routine, have you thought about the hour before you go to bed as well? According to a recent UK survey, the average person in the UK misses out on the recommended daily amount of sleep by at least 100.6 minutes, something I am definitely guilty of. In the hour before I go to bed, instead of spending the crucial moments before I nod off on my phone, I have trained myself to relax by reading with a dim light and wearing my blue light blocking glasses, with a chamomile tea next to me.

Your morning and evening routine may look completely different to mine, and that's okay. Your routines could mean finding time every evening to read, exercise or even meditate before you hit the sheets. There is no doubt that meditation can help you let go of the things cluttering up space in your

You can't serve the world if you're not serving yourself first.

head. Meditation might not be a part of my daily routine but whenever I am feeling particularly stretched, I turn to the Calm app and look up a guided meditation to help me experience a shift in state, or I listen to the Smart Girl Tribe meditation.

Whatever routine works for you is the right routine for you. It's a personal practice and there isn't one "right" way to routine, it is just an opportunity to focus on your needs.

BOUNDARIES

Now here comes the big stuff . . . One huge change I have made to improve my self-care is setting boundaries.

A whopping 48% of women say their burnout is so extreme it keeps them up at night, and before Ireland I was one of that group. Think of yourself as a bank account. Every minute or hour that you are spending on others you are taking out money, and you need to fill that bank account back up or you will go overdrawn – burnout. When you indulge in self-care you are depositing cash into your account. Once you view your time/energy as an asset that is limited, you recognize your self-care as a string of intentional habits that you need to implement to live a happier and healthier life. Setting boundaries is a crucial part of establishing a strong mental health and wellbeing.

According to psychologist Dana Nelson, "healthy boundaries are a crucial component of self-care, poor boundaries lead to resentment, anger and burnout". Firstly, you have to examine the boundaries that are currently lacking from your life. Are others too dependent on you? Do you say yes to too many commitments? If the boundaries you lack are personal then don't be shy in saying to your family or partner, "I need some time for myself today after work." If your boundaries are loose in the office, be confident in asking for help.

As women this is difficult, but we need to work harder to ask for support where needed, to delegate as necessary and to refine our workload to prioritize the long-term needs of our business and career. If you're feeling fraught at the level of social demands then decide that for every two commitments to which you are invited, you will politely decline one. Don't spread yourself too thin, sister.

I divide my boundaries into sub-categories: my personal boundaries, physical boundaries and spiritual boundaries, then it is easy to view them as boundaries for my mind, body and soul.

PERSONAL BOUNDARIES (BOUNDARIES FOR THE MIND)
If you are an empath like me you will hold on to someone else's misfortune. I have spent nights weeping over another's grief, tearing myself up about someone else's anger and

writing about other people's issues in my journal as though they are mine to bear.

Being empathetic isn't a bad thing, an empath is compassionate in regard to someone else's feelings and is subsequently able to give great advice. On the other hand, if you were to come into my office and talk to me about all the stresses bothering you, that is emotion I will take home with me, stress that I allow to become mine as well. Like anything else, there has to be a happy balance. I have learned how to shield myself from letting other people's problems or situations stick to me in the following ways.

I say *no* more frequently to event invitations, nights out and even coffee dates I know will be an hour of a friend analysing every former relationship she has ever been in.

This might not work for everyone but on The Ashley Hann Show podcast, I heard the actress, businesswoman and author Elena Cardone advise that in a relationship you should see yourselves as Queen and King (or Queen and Queen, or King and King). What does this mean? Well, you wouldn't catch a Queen venting to her "handmaidens" about her intimate issues or personal annoyances about the King, would you? Just as you wouldn't hear a King being spiteful to the jester about the Queen. This really gave me a different perspective.

If I ever have a problem with my partner, I talk to him about it and only him. Of course, sometimes a catch-up with my girlfriends over wine can help diffuse any frustration I am feeling but I don't vent, rant or share anything with a friend or stranger that would make him feel uncomfortable. It is you and your partner versus the problem, not you versus your partner. This also means that you don't find too much of my partner on my personal Instagram feed, for no other reason than our relationship is sacred to me, a partnership I want to protect.

When we don't have strong boundaries in our personal life, we can find ourselves in an unhealthy or toxic relationship. (Did you know that one in three women experiences a toxic relationship in her lifetime?) A relationship should be a union of equals. If your partner makes you feel as though you're always "wrong", no matter how hard you try, you'll never be enough to please your partner. You need to leave any relationship, whether romantic or platonic, that makes you feel as though you're not worthy or that you are less than the other person. Building your self-worth and your self-care will help you to more easily distinguish toxic relationship behaviour.

I've been there; I once turned to my toxic ex and said: "My purpose – the reason why I am here on the planet – is to save you." I know, don't you just cringe reading that? The CEO of a female empowerment organization, and still my self-worth was so low that I fundamentally believed I was here for him.

Check in with yourself before checking in on the world.

It was a relationship that gave me panic attacks and made me question myself constantly, and it was only when I came out of that relationship that I realized that his behaviour had been destructive, but *I* had allowed it to happen. My self-respect wasn't strong enough to recognize that the mental and emotional abuse was unacceptable.

With regards to work boundaries, if your job is in an office environment, know that pushing yourself too hard is only going to lead to breaking point. My friend Katherine, when starting out in her career, worked for a music production company as an intern. A few weeks in, she called me crying from the office cubicle. "I can't take it anymore!" she sobbed. I couldn't believe it; only a few hours prior she had been telling me how appreciative she was for this privileged opportunity. I begged her to take her lunch hour to come and meet me. The dewy, determined friend of mine had turned almost grey – she had lost all her energy and spark.

See, as an intern, Katherine was always the last soldier standing and took on the brunt of the work. Others were able to enforce their working hours and leave on time by passing jobs to Katherine. To get things finished she was staying late and getting in early. She felt powerless, but I reminded her it was because she had given away her power: Whether you are starting out or at the top, everyone is entitled to limits. I advised she talk firstly to the team she worked with and, as a result, she was no longer burdened with all the additional tasks. I'm no fool though, not every office will be like this.

If you need to implement stronger boundaries in the office I would suggest creating structure and set boundaries at home first. For example, have one work and one personal phone, or one work computer and one for personal admin. "If you don't want colleagues and clients to contact you at all hours, verbally tell them the hours you will be available for work-related conversations," says Julie De Azevedo Hanks, author of *The Burnout Cure.*

Equally, in this example, Katherine needed her own boundaries around the rest of her team, who had established their own. Don't be shy to have that conversation.

PHYSICAL BOUNDARIES (BOUNDARIES FOR YOUR BODY)
Another boundary you need to address is the relationship you have with your body. It can be all too easy to jump on a diet bandwagon and push yourself to your limits, then as soon as we start liking a part of ourselves that we previously didn't, we find something new to worry about. Now, I won't be sharing my ways for you to stay fit but I will urge you to implement a boundary around body positivity – we all need to feel positive about our physical self and treat it with care and respect. The relationship you have with yourself will

dominate all of your boundaries – you will change your job, and your circle of friends will alter over time but you only get one body.

Instead of jumping on the scales and being specific or telling yourself to drop a whole dress size or becoming fixated with measurements, implement a boundary and let yourself live free. Life is to be lived – don't tie your worth to a digit or dress size. Remember when I was on that beach in Italy and how much I missed out on? Because I didn't have a boundary around my perception of my body, I kept mentally beating myself up over and over – my Sheila was talking – until the sun came down and I was on my journey home. One thing that helps is reminding myself that I exercise to celebrate my body and to see how powerful and resilient it can be.

SPIRITUAL BOUNDARIES (BOUNDARIES FOR YOUR SOUL)
Negative feelings and emotions – whether from your own situation or someone else's – can take up residence in your whole body. This is exactly why after long days I indulge in spiritual self-care, which typically for me means visualization and breathwork.

Everything in our world is energy. We are surrounded by it and carry it in ourselves too. As an empath, I take on other people's negative feelings. To help protect my energy before

I go into a stressful or chaotic environment – if a friend calls me wanting to talk about her bad day or I have a meeting with a difficult and negative person – I metaphorically shield myself. I visualize a soft pink orbit protecting me from any negativity. I have heard of others who envision a white light but for me nothing can penetrate a pink light shield other than love and compassion.

I have always been aware of the power in breathwork, especially when travelling. When I was island hopping around Greece, the only way to travel from Skiathos to Alonnisos was by ferry, and that's when I realized how much of a terrible traveller I can be. Even thinking back now makes me a little queasy. The journey was four hours long and I was practically green by the end of it. It was so hot as we weren't allowed up on deck or to open windows, and it was terribly crowded. I tried raising my legs (apparently this helps) and closing my eyes but nothing made a difference. Then, there in the middle of a ferry, I mentally checked out. I had headphones on and I purely focused on my breathing: in for four long counts, and out for four counts. Over and over again. There were tourists leaning over me, children running around dodging me and a megaphone practically in my ear telling me about the sights in Alonnisos to look forward to, but I was vacant. I never knew until then how significant breathing could be. Even now, I will put on a calm song or meditation and take in a deep breath

I have always been
committed to
living as my best
self and that has
meant changing
my habits, because
habits strung
together become
your days, which in
turn become your
months, then years,
which become your
destiny.

until it fills my stomach and then slowly exhale over and over again when I need to find space in my life.

My burnout and break-up made me realize how much I was taking on, professionally and mentally, to the point that I had been just going through the motions. I was showing up as my best self, my work was great and I seemed to be successful but I didn't feel like that inside. I felt completely detached from my goals and the person I was destined to become.

Using visualization has made me think specifically about my life and where I, and the business, are heading. Visualizing is a way of "playing" your life in your head – exactly as you want your life to look like in the future. Even as a CEO of a business, I have down days and moments when I question myself. On those days I come back to the core of my vision and I close my eyes and envisage where I want to be heading. Really focusing on how I would feel if x, y and z came true and visualizing that moment as if it were real is a tactic many of my mentors have used for years. It harnesses the power of our subconscious mind.

Picture the future as though you have already achieved your goal. Imagine the scene in as much detail as possible: where are you? What are you wearing? What emotions are you feeling? Who is with you? Spend 15 minutes visualizing the scene of your triumph and eliminate any doubts that come to you. Carry any feelings you have with you throughout your day.

The great thing about visualization is you only need yourself to do it. Taking even just five minutes to connect with yourself on a deeper level and ask yourself what it would feel like if your dream was realized is a powerful mental exercise to boost your energy and spiritual health.

VALUES

Our core values make it easier for us to navigate our lives and priorities, they are the inner guide that underpins our key decisions and behaviours. It is a term we can find difficult to define, but understanding and strengthening your values will help you to develop greater self-worth. Collect and list all of the values that fit you, perhaps communication or respect, endurance or creativity, kindness or fun – look up a list online to help you to select those that best fit you. I have three core values (I wouldn't want my list to be endless): grace, authenticity and strength. Values can grow and change with us, and it is not always possible to live close to our values, especially when we are younger and still working out what is most important to us. Your job might not be representative of your core values, or perhaps you feel out of kilter with your values in certain relationships or friendships. Facing any pain or hardship, or even just life in general, is going to demand different versions of you, but your values should be seamless in each sector of your life.

Grace is my primary value. To me, living a life of grace means living a more candid actuality. Grace is a force we can tap into whenever we so desire, it is having the wisdom to take the high road. Even though I am the CEO of Smart Girl Tribe, I practise as much grace in the office as I do at home.

How exactly did I come up with this definition of my value? My self-care year started two months before New Year's Eve, and on that celebration at midnight I was searching for one word that would encompass everything I was trying to achieve through my self-care year. It came to me – grace for myself, grace for others and grace for pesky situations that would arise because, no matter what year it is, this is the game of life and there will always be problems.

We are always presented with opportunities in our lives to make conscious decisions about who we are going to be and how we are going to handle situations. I hold on to the profound belief that I can move through challenges by making choices based on my highest potential. By living a life that is built on your own personal values you will attract friends with whom you share those core values. My closest friends are some of the most gracious people I have met, and I can wholeheartedly say that the collaborations I have had since my self-care year, and being gracious in everything I do, have developed into some of the most beautiful partnerships.

I live through that word "grace". I ask myself how my best self – Super Scarlett, my most gracious self – would react to this. Remember the girl from high school who sent me a DM on my birthday, whom I mentioned earlier, and I responded with kindness? *That* was grace. On a daily basis, I never respond to road rage, for example, or to big things that happen to me professionally and personally.

A few years ago, one of the UK's largest glossy magazines started reaching out to Smart Girl Tribe writers under the premise that they wanted to connect. It was actually an underhand way to find out about the inner workings of Smart Girl Tribe. Only a few months later I bumped into the editor who had set up those meetings, and even though I was upset that my writers were being contacted under false information, I introduced myself and responded with grace. Grace isn't always easy. It's a muscle, one we have to work at every day to make strong and it will often be in the most challenging times when we will be required to use it.

Self-care is
ultimately about
giving yourself
the space to build
an exceptional
relationship with
your body, your
environment and
yourself.

SELF-WORTH

Remember that your self-worth is determined by your values. We all have a tendency to measure our self-worth against our accomplishments and achievements – remember those words I hate – *if* and *when*. I will be more loveable *if* I lose weight, I will be happier *when* I am promoted, which in turn will make my parents even prouder of me.

Here is a tool I use to remind myself of my self-worth and what I have to offer the world.

EXERCISE: PORTFOLIO YOUR ACCOLADES

We all have to-do lists of what we want to get done and achieve, but how often do we look back and think of everything we have successfully completed, the dreams that we have already realized?

On stages, I share the importance of self-care beyond the cliché Pinterest quotes. One of my favourite ways to practise self-care has been putting together a portfolio of my achievements or accolades.

Being so focused on the future, I rarely look back on everything I have done. However, sitting down and adding to my scrapbook-type portfolio helps me stay confident and motivated. Munroe Bergdorf, the activist and trailblazer, told me that this is one of the most effective ways to cheer yourself up on off days. I followed her advice and in my office now have three scrapbooks filled with everything from career mementos and photos from the first time I was invited to speak at Harvard University as a female empowerment expert, to written letters from tribers telling us how much we are helping them, and certificates and magazine articles about Smart Girl Tribe.

Sometimes, I totally am the girl to enjoy the bath salts and a session of meditation, but at other times self-care is being present and feeling good about myself which is exactly what my portfolio does for me.

As you enter the world of self-love there will be some behaviours and people that try to throw you off track. Over the years I have had positive and negative relationships with Instagram. One day I saw on my feed how many people I was following with whom I didn't have a direct relationship or connection so I unfollowed everyone not serving or inspiring me. It wasn't that their posts prompted negative emotions in me, but spending hours each day scrolling through them was taking over my life and diverting me from my purpose, maybe even costing me my destiny.

Accepting and loving yourself are two critical ingredients to being comfortable in your own skin and they go hand in hand. Of course, it has never been so hard to be authentic, as now we are literally able to become anyone or anything. When you love yourself, you have the power to handle any situation with integrity and respect.

ADMIT WHEN YOU'RE HAVING A BAD DAY

There will be triumphs, tribulations, tears and tests as you move through life, especially when you are as ambitious and stubborn as I am. Before I travelled to Ireland, I couldn't even admit to myself, let alone anyone else, when I was going through tough times.

Part of feeling worthy is trusting yourself and your own judgement (some call this sixth sense, gut instinct or intuition). When you have a decision to make, do what *you* think is right and know in your heart to be true, and be proud of that. Stop arguing against yourself, stop highlighting your flaws and selling yourself short. If you are still finding it hard to get to grips with this, turn back to read about your inner mean girl again.

When you set a goal, follow through with it and don't give yourself excuses to walk away or give up. Vow to keep every promise you make to yourself. We can get so busy and think:

"It's fine, we will do it tomorrow, or some day soon." Hello – "someday" isn't a day. Check the calendar, it won't be there.

When you decide on one thing you are going to do for yourself, keep to the pledge, however small it is. Breaking promises is self-sabotaging. You wouldn't let a friend down by breaking a promise, would you? Bet on yourself, back your own plan.

THE POWER OF KINDNESS

If you're coming to understand the concept of what self-love can do to transform your life, let's take a moment to think about what giving to others can give to your own life.

While on a Tanzanian safari, which has been the greatest experience of my life so far. We witnessed the big five, greeted the Maasai tribe and slept in an outside tent where lions ran and zebra gathered around us throughout the nights.

One moment, however, stood out for me. On our last stop of the week, our truck driver Ally pulled up to show us the magnificent wooden creations his friend spends months crafting. The business was set up in a makeshift shelter, surrounded by beautiful wooden giraffes and elephants and I noticed two young girls smiling and waving excitedly at me. One was as young as seven and was carrying and caring for her eight-month-old brother in her arms. Their clothes were worn, and they had no shoes, but that didn't matter. They had the most radiant smiles and it was impossible for me to suppress my overwhelming emotion. These children had nothing yet they were still smiling and caring for one another. They didn't compare themselves with us, weren't sad or revelling in the amenities or possessions they didn't have, but were focused on what they did have – each other.

We hugged and laughed together and, through gestures, conversed brokenly. Even though I gave them money, it wasn't that that delighted them. The one treat I had to offer was some bars of chocolate stashed away in my backpack from breakfast that morning. The children were overjoyed at the sight of it, and luckily I had enough for everyone. They licked their lips and thanked me profusely – something that for so many years I had taken completely for granted. (No, not chocolate, but kindness.) I didn't have anything to give but money or this tasty delight. I gave them both, and willingly. Pulling myself back onto the truck as Ally said we had to leave, they all waved at me gloriously, with chocolate wrappers everywhere, and they started dancing and wishing me well.

During a time we can be anything, why not be kind? Have you ever kept something hidden because you've been scared or worried about what other people would think? For one friend of mine it was an eating disorder, for a colleague of mine it was self-harming. My friends only opened up to me when I told them about the importance of the act of kindness.

If you *have* ever hidden something, what makes you think the person next to you hasn't either? Everyone you meet is fighting battles you know nothing about so be empathetic. Always help someone because you might be the only one that does. This could be calling a friend to check in with them, smiling at a passer-by or picking up someone else's groceries for them. The reason why kindness is so great is because it's free and touches lives. It's the thing that brings us together.

I love Christmas and I have no doubt that I am even kinder around this time. That's one reason why I love it so much, because everyone becomes even more thoughtful and giving at this time of year. But kindness isn't a trend, and it shouldn't be treated like a fad; it should be an all-year, every-day-long act.

"People are like stained-glass windows. They sparkle and shine when the sun is out, but when the darkness sets in their true beauty is revealed only if there is light from within."

— Elisabeth Kübler-Ross

Smart Girl Tribe has flourished as a result of my commitment to kindness. From the beginning, my mission has been for women to be kinder to each other, but in order to achieve that we have to be kinder to ourselves. The platform featured the conversations that weren't being discussed in mainstream media, but we also made a special effort to celebrate women around the world achieving awe-inspiring things, and shared ideas to help women love themselves more.

In a world that is encouraging us to be strong, resilient and tough, kindness is often a characteristic that is overlooked and underestimated. Being kind can be small and large, and can mean generosity or respect. It's important to take into account all of our differences, whether that be our race, socio-economic background or faith. That is how we can grow, by recognizing our differences and appreciating everyone for who they are and what they can bring to the table.

Growing up, people would try to label me, just as much as people would have tried, I am sure, to label you. The two words "I AM" are powerful and accessible to all. We just need the bravery to define what comes after that, whatever it is – to enable everyone to see the most glorious version of you.

Imagine how the world would look if everyone chose to be the grace and the kindness in someone else's day. Lord knows, my friends and partner, even family members can be embarrassed to be seen out with me. Why? Because I express exactly what I am thinking in the moment. How good does it feel when someone takes time out of their day to tell you they love your outfit? Or even to smile? I regularly notice how often we do that on nights out, and in bathrooms when we bump into another woman, it's like a hiding place, away from societal expectations and pressures when we all start finally embracing each other. Which is why I always speak the truth. I'm never too shy to walk up to complete strangers in bars or restaurants to share how much I love their look. That is exactly what we could use more of – genuine kindness, especially as women – a few lines to say "I see you".

***

We live in a culture where we focus on romantic love and what we can receive or, equally, what we can give our partners. The most meaningful and important long-term relationship you will ever have, though, is the one you have with yourself.

If you are obsessed with sketching, then spend quality time with yourself doing it. If you love having dinner out, do it. Wake up, friend – you are "the one". Like any relationship it will take work and effort and care. Make yourself the priority. Wear something fun that makes you feel incredible. Give yourself

By not being where you *thought* you should be, you might end up exactly where you're supposed to go.

a thoughtful gift of flowers, sweets, a new playlist or a cute necklace. Celebrate your milestones and small victories, and don't stint on your self-care system.

Our downtime and rest prepare us to be at our best when we strive to reach our dreams. To be kind to others, to give to others and to reach the peak of your capability you have to first be kind to yourself, give to yourself and love yourself.

SMART GIRL ACTIONS

- Practise your Morning Prompts to help build a morning routine that inspires positivity and balance in your daily life.
- I love the Portfolio Your Accolades exercise – it's such a brilliant way of collecting together a valuable tool to demonstrate your values and worth.
- Develop a routine. My morning and evening routines are sacred (you will find them online at smartgirltribe. com if you search for "my evening happiness routine" and "my morning happiness routine"). Carve out time dedicated for yourself either in the morning or evening.
- I use mirrors to reflect the person I want to be, my sticky notes on my mirror are full of positive affirmations so when I am getting ready, I feel inspired and uplifted.

CHAPTER 8

I PROMISE TO STAND UP AND HELP CHANGE THE WORLD

Zendaya, Jacinda Ardern, Margaret Atwood. Have you ever fan-girled so hard for someone that you knew deep down you couldn't possibly meet them? Years ago I was invited to a charity gala and the room was full of celebrities. I could tell you now that I wasn't nervous or intimidated, but my nose bleed would tell you different. The anxiety had literally gone straight to my head. I was the girl in a slinky ballgown, having had my hair and make-up done, lying down in a bathroom stall with my legs above my head and drabs of tissue up my nose.

Among the obvious celebrities, there have been politicians, activists, authors and experts I have admired both near and far for years. The greatest being Helen Pankhurst, the great-granddaughter of Emmeline Pankhurst, the prominent British suffragette. In 2018 my work led me to being invited to the

Houses of Parliament to advocate for equality in politics. Throughout the day there, I met my local councillor, spoke with aspiring activists and there, as I was having my photo taken with the 50:50 Parliament team, in the corner stood Helen Pankhurst. Would my nose prevail? As I scurried over, there was no sign of blood yet. My mind was foggy. I was the CEO of what organization? Built it at what age? At first, I was tongue-tied and nervous but once I had found my groove our conversation was coherent.

Maybe you are yet to find the cause that ignites you, so I ask you: have you ever felt as though you have no power? That nobody would listen to you? Have you ever been referred to as "little girl"? Me too.

Smart Girl Tribe began because I was determined to help change the narrative for women. I could easily have left Smart Girl Tribe to someone else, thinking that my voice is too quiet or that I am too much of an introvert. Here is the thing though – even if your voice shakes, it's imperative that you use it.

Making change could be raising money for those less fortunate or helping at a homeless or domestic violence shelter. It could be building schools in the developing world or encouraging your peers with hashtags on social media. Young women more than ever are becoming an energized and acting transformative change, not only in our country

Your actions can change the next generation, so they can live in a better world than the one we have today, if only we'd all assume our responsibility to advocate for those who need our collective voice.

but throughout the world. We are rising to the occasion and exerting our influence and power.

Doing whatever you can to raise your voice and empower others is the driving force we still need. You don't even need access to money, luxury or power to do this. I changed the world from a dorm room with no internet connection, and you can as well. Gina Martin had no background in activism when a man took a photo up her skirt back in 2016 and she decided to take it to the government. She subsequently forced a change in the law and is now a regular campaigner. Hope Virgo started #Dumpthescales as a response to the media promotion of blemish-free and fatless models. Her campaign is based on her own experience battling anorexia. Here is how *you* can become a voice for change.

SHARE STORIES

How can you effect transformation? Firstly, and simply, you must share your story. Issues don't disappear unless we open up and reveal our narratives. If we don't talk about them, we cannot fully deal with them. By sharing, we learn that we are not alone, and we are united in our insecurities; that we are all human. By sharing your story you are unlocking someone else's prison.

Being an NSPCC ambassador, I have met so many inspiring children. I am in awe of those who stand up against bullying, are growing up in foster care, or are living through the issues we at Smart Girl Tribe are fighting against. They are the proof that all of our stories matter, that nobody deserves a voice to go unheard. It is our histories and experiences that unite us, no matter our appearance, how old we are or who we love. Storytelling is the most universal tool we can use to resonate with each other and make change. It connects us and allows us to start conversations. No matter what you are doing, everything is storytelling, whether you're a musician, an artist or even a lawyer.

You may think your story isn't compelling enough to share, or perhaps you choose not to open up. Don't underestimate how much change you can have by shining a light on someone else's story then. I am a staunch advocate for women's rights but I also fight for sustainability and the black community, among other endeavours. Being socially conscious is more than a hashtag, it's more than language; it is a state of mind, and realization that society doesn't treat everyone equally.

Ipsos Mori found that 42 per cent of young people aged between 10 and 20 had participated in some kind of meaningful social action in the last year, which is fantastic. Think about your talents and skills and how to best serve the causes close to your heart and use every opportunity to learn. This is going to deepen your commitment and will also build roots. It's like a slice of cake. If everyone brings a small slice to the party, how many cakes will there be? Hundreds. And that's what social change is: hundreds of small actions coming together.

EXERCISE: SKILL UP

Activism isn't just a social media campaign or hashtag, it is about making real change and having a positive impact. It requires you talking to people you have never met before and educating yourself about your chosen issue.

Maybe there is a protest you want to be part of or a campaign you want to share on social media but you don't know where or how to start. List three skills you are great at. Are you a good problem solver? Do you love speaking to large crowds? Does your skill lie in communication or writing or researching? Figure out how you can bring these skills to the campaign or problem you are passionate about.

With campaigns I support, I prefer to work face to face with the organization and ask how I can help.

When I was based abroad in Amsterdam, there was a UN campaign I was particularly interested in – the Draw The Line campaign which saw celebrities such as Billie Piper draw a line to stress the importance of ending sexual violence. Being abroad, using social media was the only method I had to get involved so I asked the organization to take part, they instantly agreed and it was a small victory upon my return when I saw the campaign in the cinema for the first time. Decide what skills you have, and what you can contribute most significantly. How can you serve with excellence?

BE INCLUSIVE

To make change, you also need to be inclusive. Ask yourself: does everyone in my story look the same? You don't need to change your faith, belief or bank balance to fit with everyone, but you need to do life with those who don't look like or vote like you, to add new hues and dialogues. Every morning you get to choose how you want your world to appear.

Living with unconscious bias will impact your children, your family, your work and your community. When there isn't a seat at the table, pull up your own chair and bring a megaphone to help other women share their stories. Make sure your table is full of different ethnicities, perspectives and backgrounds. Guys are amazing too, they deserve a say, an opinion and a place. Embracing everyone's different stories is similar to creating a beautiful blanket full of different patchwork pieces. Wouldn't you rather have that than a standard single-colour quilt?

Being inclusive also means waking up to internalized and institutional prejudices. It means allowing people to identify as they do, whether that's woman, man, gender fluid or otherwise, and the same for political and religious beliefs and sexual orientation. Some will identify with labels, other won't. Fill your educational circle with a variety of people so you can walk away with the benefits of diversity. At the back of the book you will find a list of resources I highly recommend.

LOOK AROUND
Thirdly, if you really want to be a change-maker then look around you. I became an advocate for females because I was watching those in higher and stronger positions than me who should have been doing better but weren't. I couldn't pass on the baton, so I took it and ran. There was a huge need for a female empowerment organization that would show women the alternative to how they've been living.

Activism has always been a part of my life; it didn't just happen with Smart Girl Tribe. For me it was a natural interest rather than a career path at first. Even if you don't feel like an instinctive campaigner, there will be things you want to change around you. For example, I started an international organization at my high school which is still running today.

Passing on the message and spreading the word is enough too. Maybe you don't have the funds to donate money, but you can find someone who does. The most important thing is you just *do*. When I first talked to a group of young girls who have endured some of life's worst challenges and tribulations with the NSPCC, I knew the game was on. They were looking up to me and I had to show up for them. Seeing their faces as they shared their stories with others in the group, encouraging each other and telling each other to fight, was the change I needed to see in the world. Nobody could pay me enough to leave this job, receiving emails and messages every single day telling me how encouraging Smart Girl Tribe is means everything.

Consider volunteering to network and gain experience. By helping an organization you admire, you learn more about your chosen cause. Young people are the key to our future. Helping others through volunteering from a young age is enriching and can also help you to work on your self-esteem and confidence. Google local volunteering opportunities, or just contact the closest Oxfam or foodbank.

Before you go out in the world, read, watch documentaries and listen to podcasts about something you are passionate about. You might think you haven't got a particular cause, and that's perfectly okay too. Not everyone needs one particular topic. Find something you disagree with – perhaps the pink tax, or something bigger such as eating meat. It can also be as small as a tree in your community being dug up. Learn what you can about your cause to give you the knowledge you need to educate others and ignite change. Don't be so ill-informed that when someone listens to you your facts don't back up your cause, or you don't have enough evidence.

Giving back starts with a choice: attending a party you don't want to go to when you have been asked to by a friend, babysitting, volunteering at the local library, helping at a homeless shelter over the holidays or committing to purchasing only beauty products not tested on animals. All this is activism. It all contributes to shaping the world and making it a better place. Imagine if every woman reading this helped just one other person? How many people would have their lives changed? Thousands.

> *"How wonderful it is that nobody needs wait a single moment before starting to improve the world."*
>
> **— Anne Frank**

EXERCISE: LISTEN UP

One thing that stops many of us from making change is that we don't listen, or we listen mindlessly. When was the last time you really heard what someone was saying to you? Teach yourself how to be not just a good listener, but a great one. It takes practice.

Ask yourself before speaking to someone, "What is one thing I can take away from this? What can I learn from this conversation?"

Then, when you walk away, ask yourself what you learned about yourself from meeting or conversing with that person. What did you learn about other people? What did you learn about the world? What can you do *now*?

Start testing yourself in this way, and your world will open up and you'll meet more interesting people because of it. That is where the magic happens – life is about connection, and *real* connection. You will only bond with someone on a human level if you truly hear them and their story, if you understand what makes them tick. It will seem strange at first asking yourself questions straight after walking away from someone, but I promise it will help you – and the world.

USE SOCIAL MEDIA

You now have a megaphone in your hands. Social media has transformed the way we communicate and is such a powerful tool for activists. There are a wealth of fruitful connections to be made on your platform of choice, and you can search and find individuals and organizations that share the same values and goals as you do.

Our culture is obsessed with follows and likes, but engagement is key. Take pride in how people are connecting with you and who you are virtually meeting over how well your post is rating.

Social media has revolutionized the way we fight for social justice and we have to get on board. So many modern-day reform campaigns start with hashtag activism, shifting the dialogue surrounding important issues such as sexism and racism. The next step is to take the activism out of our connectable devices and make important causes tangible.

"Activism is a need to know, a need to explain and a need to help."

— Rowan Blanchard

The woman who wants to move the world has to move herself first. She has to change the world through acts and behaviour which, sister, you are doing just by reading this book. There is one underlying principle to improving the world that all smart girls stick to: that is, resisting wrongful acts through love and kindness. For more happiness, be happy to everyone you meet; for more compassion, show compassion to those around you; for peace in the world, live in peace starting today.

Our world's future isn't written yet. We can design a new narrative, one that doesn't focus on struggle but on progress. Start by having smarter conversations and really listening. Personally, I have always been attracted to storytelling around women's lives and highlighting those underrepresented voices. I need you to be as well. The world is being schooled, and the teachers are the youth.

SMART GIRL ACTIONS

- Skill up – decide what skills you choose to develop so that you can support change where it is needed.
- Listen up – information is key to understanding how and what you can do to make a difference.
- Engage in a social platform. Not all of us have the opportunity to protest and march. I spent my teenage years in rural Italy, far from the city, so I never experienced face-to-face activism. If you are in a similar position, then social media is a great tool. Look into accounts that have a positive impact on the world or search for petitions on Change.org that you can share on Facebook.
- Consciously practise what you preach.
- Invite those who need it to your party. Some refer to it as pie, I refer it to it as a party. To make up a pie or party, you need lots of different slices or people. You need those with different strengths who believe in one core message. Once you have decided on the cause or causes you want to fight for, seek out those who can help spread your message. Connect with them and interview them; find out how you can shine a light on your message even more.

MY LETTER TO YOU

Dear reader, sister, listener, friend...

The truth is that no matter what I am pursuing or building – the event series, the podcast, the programmes or this book – it is to help you understand that everything you need to be the woman you are destined to be, to achieve that audacious dream, is already inside you. You have always had it inside you. You are the hero of your life, the leading lady.

As women we have a tendency to seek validation or permission outside ourselves; we wait for others to encourage and push us to achieve our dreams. I want you to reread the Smart Girl promises regularly, and remember that you can make it happen. Being a Smart Girl means unconditionally loving yourself, in spite of your mistakes, trauma and the mean girls you've encountered. It's living beyond the societal standards and instead committing to being your super self and taking the action required to make those wild dreams happen. Hold yourself accountable when you are spending too much time caring about other people's opinions or your social media presence.

Nothing will make you happier than doing what you love, so dare to dream big, dare to love yourself deeply, dare to be bold, to be *you*, the beautiful, worthy, unique you. Dare to be the Smart Girl and redefine the impossible.

I had nothing more than you do. I am just the girl who decided to go for it, just as you can.

Love
Scarlett x

ACKNOWLEDGEMENTS

Thank you:

To my parents, to my core I could never thank you enough for your unwavering support and faith in my dreams. You cultivated a space for me to redefine the impossible.

To my brothers Tobias and Austen. It is the greatest honour being your sister, I love you.

To Lauren, Jo, Kate and the entire Trigger team; thank you for bringing my vision to life, you are fierce representations of smart women. What a tribe we have become.

To my team, the originals who connected with me on Twitter all those years ago just hoping to be part of a movement that would change the narrative for women, and to my current team members who grow and build this media powerhouse with me every single day and continuously fight the good fight.

Finally, my most important thank you – to you, reader. May this book help your journey towards becoming the woman you are destined to be. Whether you are a reader, listener, viewer or event attendee, you make up Smart Girl Tribe. We are bonded for life and I sincerely hope you close this book knowing you are enough, that any dream can come true and you're never alone – I am here.

RESOURCES

BOOKS

Barmash, I, *The Self-Made Man: Success and Stress American Style* (Beard Books, 2003)

Beasley, M, *The Eleanor Roosevelt Encyclopedia* (Greenwood Publishing Group, 2001)

Bernhardt, K, *The Anxiety Cure: Live a Life Free From Panic In Just a Few Weeks* (Vermilion, 2018)

Covey, S, *7 Habits of Highly Effective People* (Free Press, 1989)

Green, C, *She Means Business* (Hay House, 2017)

Hanks, J, *The Burnout Cure: An Emotional Survival Guide for Overwhelmed Women* (Covenant Communications, 2013)

Hay, L, *You Can Heal Your Life* (Hay House, 1984)

Johnson, J, *WorkParty* (Gallery Books, 2018)

Kaplan, J, *The Gratitude Diaries: How a Year Looking on the Bright Side Can Transform your Life* (Hachette, 2015)

Mannes, E, *The Power of Music* (Walker & Company, 2011)

Robbins, A, *Awaken the Giant Within* (Simon & Schuster UK, 1991)

REFERENCES

Agyei, S, "Passion Is Energy. Feel The Power That Comes From Focusing On What Excites You," Medium, 2015

Bonas, C, "Fear Itself with Cressida Bonas" [podcast], 2019

Day, E, "How to Fail with Elizabeth Day" [podcast], 2018

"Drawaline", UN Women UK, 2017

"Generation Z – Beyond Binary: new insights into the next generation", Ipsos Mori, 2018

Gifford, B, "Am I being bullied? 3 types of bullying adults face", Counselling Directory, 2018

Hann, A, "Elena Cardone: Be a Queen & Build Your Empire", The Ashley Hann Show, 2019

"How Burnout Affects Women", WellRight, 2019

Korb, A, "The Grateful Brain", Psychology Today, 2012

Ma, J, "25 Friendship Quotes to Share With a Best Field", The Cut, 2018

Mapes, D, "Toxic Friends? 8 in 10 people endure poisonous pals", Today, 2011

Morsella, E, Godwin, C A, "Homing In On Consciousness In The Nervous System: An Action-Based Synthesis", *Behavioural and Brain Sciences,* Cambridge University Press, 2016

"Mental Disorders", [report], World Health Organization, 2019

Nelson, D, "Self-Care 101: Setting Healthy Boundaries", Inner Journeys Counseling, 2016

Stanton, B, "How To Create a Calming Space in Your Home", Smart Girl Tribe, 2020

Tupper, H and Ellis, S, "The Squiggly Career" [podcast], Amazing If, 2018

"UK 2018 Sleep Survey & Statistics", Chemist4U, 2019

Vukova, C, "73+ Surprising Networking Statistics To boost Your Career", Review42.com, 2020

Winfrey, O, "Dr. Brené Brown on Joy: It's Terrifying", Oprah Winfrey Network, 2013

Young, Laura, "Kicking The Plastic Habit", TEDx Talks, 2019

MENTAL HEALTH ORGANIZATIONS

Beat, www.beateatingdisorders.org.uk

Calm, www.calm.com

Fix The Glitch, www.fixtheglitch.org

Heads Together, www.headstogether.org.uk

Mind, www.mind.org.uk

Samaritans, www.samaritans.org

SANE, www.sane.org.uk

The Shaw Mind Foundation, www.shawmind.org

Time to Change, www.time-to-change.org.uk

OTHER ORGANIZATIONS

50:50 – A campaign lobbying to achieve gender-balanced parliament, www.5050parliament.co.uk

Break The Cycle – A charity supporting young people to build healthy relationships, breakthecycle.org

HeforShe – A solidarity movement for the advancement of gender equality, initiated by the United Nations, www.heforshe.org

NSPCC – The UK's leading children's charity, preventing abuse and helping those affected to recover, www.nspcc.org.uk

Prince's Trust – A youth charity that helps young people under 30 to get into jobs, education and training, www.princes-trust.org.uk

SmartWorks – A fashion and coaching service to help women get into employment, www.smartworks.org.uk

The Bully Project – A social action campaign supporting the film, *Bully*, thebullyproject.com

Women for Women International – Helps women survivors of war rebuild their lives, www.womenforwomen.org.uk

UN Women – Global champion for gender equality, www.unwomen.org

SMART GIRL TRIBE
Website: www.smartgirltribe.com
Facebook: Smart Girl Tribe
Instagram: @smartgirltribe
Podcast: 'The Smart Girl Tribe Podcast' available on Podbean, Spotify, iTunes and anywhere you can find podcasts.
The Smart Girl Tribe Summit: www.smartgirltribe.com/events

We also have wonderful bonuses and resources, especially tailored to you, to accompany this book, at smartgirltribe.com/shop. The Smart Girls Handbook programme is brimming with audio and video content as well as workbooks, designed with you in mind.

TriggerHub.org is one of the most elite and scientifically proven forms of mental health intervention

Trigger Publishing is the leading independent mental health and wellbeing publisher in the UK and US. Clinical and scientific research conducted by assistant professor Dr Kristin Kosyluk and her highly acclaimed team in the Department of Mental Health Law & Policy at the University of South Florida (USF), as well as complementary research by her peers across the US, has independently verified the power of lived experience as a core component in achieving mental health prosperity. Specifically, the lived experiences contained within our bibliotherapeutic books are intrinsic elements in reducing stigma, making those with poor mental health feel less alone, providing the privacy they need to heal, ensuring they know the essential steps to kick-start their own journeys to recovery, and providing hope and inspiration when they need it most.

Delivered through TriggerHub, our unique online portal and accompanying smartphone app, we make our library of bibliotherapeutic titles and other vital resources accessible to individuals and organizations anywhere, at any time and with complete privacy, a crucial element of recovery. As such, TriggerHub is the primary recommendation across the UK and US for the delivery of lived experiences.

At Trigger Publishing and TriggerHub, we proudly lead the way in making the unseen become seen. We are dedicated to humanizing mental health, breaking stigma and challenging outdated societal values to create real action and impact. Find out more about our world-leading work with lived experience and bibliotherapy via triggerhub.org, or by joining us on:

🐦 @triggerhub_

📘 @triggerhub.org

📷 @triggerhub_